Rev. C. W. Ruth.

ENTIRE SANCTIFICATION

A SECOND BLESSING,

TOGETHER WITH

LIFE SKETCH, BIBLE READINGS AND SERMON OUTLINES,

BY

REV. C. W. RUTH.

Wipf & Stock
PUBLISHERS
Eugene, Oregon

Wipf and Stock Publishers
199 W 8th Ave, Suite 3
Eugene, OR 97401

Entire Sanctification
A Second Blessing, Together with Life Sketch, Bible Readings, and Sermon O
By Ruth, C. W.
ISBN: 1-59752-318-6
Publication date 7/28/2005
Previously published by The Christian Witness Co., 1903

INTRODUCTION.

If one has a divine message, he has it to deliver. The nature of it demands as wide a hearing as possible.

We have long known that God had given the author of this work something to say for Him.

This, as a preacher and witness, he has said to quite a remarkable degree, the country through.

But there is a more permanent form, and a wider reach for truth than by the human voice.

How multiplied and multiplying are the works on holiness. This subject is present as never in the history of the holiness movement. God is going to be heard; He is being heard.

This will prove a helpful work. God will honor its definitions. The words of the Scriptures are used and not some human substitutes. If God says Sanctification, we should. This author does.

If people consult the Table of Contents, they will see interesting topics; if they read the chapters, they will get both information and inspiration.

CHARLES J. FOWLER.

Boston, Sept. 1st, 1903.

"Follow peace with all men
AND THE SANCTIFICATION
without which no man shall see the Lord."

Heb. 12:14. R.V.

PREFACE.

This book was not written for the critic; nor is there any effort to present an exhaustive treatise of the subject herein set forth. The desire to present in a permanent form the convictions of the writer touching this subject, in the hope that they may help some hungry heart even after the writer has gone to his reward; and the burning desire to help hungry souls into the blessed experience of entire sanctification, is the only, and we trust, sufficient excuse for the publishing of this volume. The writer has never assumed the role of an author, and begs to say that much of the matter herein presented has been written hurriedly amid the discharge of pressing pastoral duties for publication in an excellent holiness journal, "*The Nazarene Messenger,*" of Los Angeles, Cal. The book is sent forth with the prayer that hungry hearts, longing for a complete deliverance from sin, may be enabled to obtain and realize the grace of entire sanctification as a second blessing, and so, not only know the doctrine, but the experience itself. Amen.

That the blessing of God may come upon every reader and that God may be glorified in the sanctification of many souls, is the earnest wish and prayer of the writer.

C. W. RUTH.

Indianapolis, Ind., Nov. 1st, 1903.

TO

Emma Josephine Ruth,

MY CONSECRATED AND DEVOTED WIFE, WHO IS TO ME A
"HELP-MEET" INDEED, THIS VOLUME IS
MOST AFFECTIONATELY

Dedicated.

CONTENTS.

ENTIRE SANCTIFICATION.

Definitions of Sanctification... 15
Six Theories of Sanctification... 21
Sanctification and Entire Sanctification........................ 27
Distinctions between Justification and Sanctification....... 31
Justification not a Half Way Work.................................. 34
Sanctification, A Second Blessing.................................. 38
That "Something.".. 41
Essentials to Sanctification 43
Sanctification includes Separation and Consecration......... 46
Why not Sanctified when Converted?.............................. 48
Eradication or Repression, Which?................................. 50
Sanctification and the Baptism of the Holy Ghost............ 52
Entire Sanctification Necessary to Entire Satisfaction...... 55
Entire Sanctification, How Obtained............................... 57
Some Benefits of Sanctification...................................... 60
Sanctification, the Cure of Unbelief................................ 62
Growing into Sanctification... 64
Sanctification and Mistakes 65
Sanctification and Holy Living...................................... 67
Sanctification and Stability 70
Sanctification and Power 72
Sanctification and Revivals 74
Witnessing to Sanctification 76
Sanctification or "Call It What You Please.".................... 79
If Sanctified, How Could a Person Sin?........................... 82
What Becomes of People Who Are Not Sanctified?........... 84
"I Cannot See Into Sanctification.".................................. 87
Darkness and Heaviness 89
The Witness of the Spirit.. 92
"Him," or "It.".. 94
Divine Guidance 96
"Sinless Perfection." 98
First Pure, then Peaceable... 100
Perfection and Growth 102
Why Men Oppose Holiness 104
Definiteness 108
Consecration and Sanctification..................................... 110
Sanctification and Personality....................................... 112
Why the Preaching of Holiness is Essential to Revivals.... 115
Some Questions Answered... 118
The Will of God.. 121
Alone With Jesus 123
Trials 125

BIBLE READINGS,

Christian Perfection 127
Heart Purity 127
Sanctification 128
Holiness 128
Passages of Scripture Suggesting the Two Experiences...... 129

CONTENTS.

SERMON OUTLINES.

Perfect Love	131
An Uttermost Salvation	133
Full Salvation	136
The Two Baptisms	139
Holiness or Hell, Which?	141
Holiness Versus Backsliding	144
Heavenly Mindedness	147
Christ, the Way	149
Secrets of Victory	152
Self Examination	155
Glorying in the Cross	158
Seeking the Face of God	160
One Thing	162
Leprosy a Type of Sin	165
Beyond the Second Veil	167
Essential Truth	170
Jesus Christ, the God-Man	172
The Test of Genuine Religion	175
Redeemed from the Curse of the Law	177

FULLNESS OF JESUS.

Hungering and Thirsting	180
Ask and Receive	180
With the Spirit	181
Above Measure	181
Filled	182
Blessings Poured Out	182
Full of Sap	183
Full of Light	183
Filled With God's Fullness	184
Filled by Faith	184
Full of Power	185
Fruits of Righteousness	185
Full of Goodness	186
Filled With Food	186
God's Fulness	187
Full of Wisdom	187
Fullness of the Blessing	188
Mouths Filled	188
Fullness of the Godhead	189
Good Measure	189
Full of Temporal Blessings	190
Filled With Knowledge	190
Full of Good Works	191
The Hungry are Filled	191
Filled With Joy	192

LIFE SKETCH.

The writer was born September 1st, 1865, in Hilltown township, Bucks county, Penna. Both my father and mother were devoted and consistent Christians, and members of the Evangelical Association before I was born, hence I grew up in a home-atmosphere of real spirituality and godliness. For this I am devoutly thankful. Among my earliest recollections are the family altar, the Sabbath School, and attendance upon the prayer meetings, revival meetings and camp meetings with my parents. I was the first-born, and only son, having three younger sisters. I do not think there ever was a day, from my earliest childhood to the time of my conversion, the Spirit of God did not strive with me, and bring to my heart conviction for sin and my need of a Savior. Often times I was "almost persuaded" to become a Christian, and always cherished the purpose to do so at some time, and yet, withal, procrastinated, and so became more and more hardened and corrupted by sin. But the consciousness that my parents were daily and constantly praying for me, often restrained me from outward sin, and kept my conscience tender. For several years I lived on the farm with my Grandparents, who also were devout Christians, and here too the influences of religion constantly surrounded and restrained me. Having but limited means, my parents were unable to provide me with any especial educational advantages. Living in a country village or on the farm, I never had the privilege of attending even a graded school, and for the most part attended a country school; and even here circumstances compelled an irregular attendance. At the age of sixteen it was decided that I should learn some trade, and so arrangements were made for me to go to a neighboring town (Quakertown, Penna.) to serve an apprenticeship in a printing office. Here again I found myself surrounded with religious influences, as the proprietor of the printing office was a Christian gentleman. In the same office with me was the son of a preacher. We became quite intimate friends. After a few months he was sent for by his father to attend a camp meeting. At once I surmised the object in view, and remarked to a fellow-workman that when the preacher's son would return from the camp meeting he would be religious. The more I thought of it, the more fully I believed it would be so, and the thought greatly distressed me. Somehow, I felt that if he was converted I would have to be. As he returned on Monday morning, just one look into his countenance, before he had uttered a word, convinced me that my fears had come true. Instantly I was in trouble, and under deep conviction. I felt there was a chasm between us. Without saying much to me upon the subject of religion, he declared his purpose to attend the mid-week prayer meeting, and insisted on my going with him; this I finally consented to do.

This was on a Friday night. Here conviction became so pungent and intense, I publicly confessed myself a seeker; after much earnest crying and agonizing prayer to God, by day and night, confessing my sins, I was gloriously converted on the following Sunday night. The pastor of the church I attended, after an earnest sermon, invited seekers to come forward to the altar of prayer. I rejoiced in the opportunity, and rushed forward to the altar, fell upon my knees, and plead for mercy. At about 9:30 o'clock, God in mercy heard my prayer, the burden of my guilt, was rolled away, the light of heaven broke into my soul, the Spirit witnessed with my spirit that I was pardoned and accepted of God, and was indeed a new creature in Christ. Although I had been averse to religious demonstrations, I now found myself shouting aloud the praises of God. I was born again and knew it. This occurred early in September, 1882. Praise God forever more! Soon after this I was baptized and united with the church.

During the following year I lived a most earnest and devoted Christian life, attending faithfully all the means of grace. I carried two testaments—one German and one English—in my pockets, and used my spare time in studying the same. Thus I maintained a clear justified experience. But I had gone only a very short time in my Christian experience until I discovered, much to my amazement, that there still remained a something in my heart that hindered me, and at times even defeated me. The principal manifestations of that "something" were, a man-fearing spirit, the uprising of an unholy temper, difficulty in forgiving and loving an enemy, etc. I learned that Jesus could remove the root of those difficulties out of the heart. Just one year after I had been so gloriously converted, while yet in my first love, I definitely sought the experience of entire sanctification. After seeking earnestly for some days, one Sunday night while walking down the side-walk toward the church, conscious that I had consecrated my all for time and eternity, I was enabled to look up into heaven, and say,

"I believe that the blood of Jesus cleanseth my heart from all sin now; He sanctifies me now," and suddenly and consciously the Holy Ghost fell upon me, and I knew just as positively and as assuredly that God had sanctified me through and through, as I had known a year before that he had pardoned my sins. I rushed into the church, and before the pastor had time to announce the opening hymn, I told the congregation what had occurred on the sidewalk, and that God had sanctified me wholly. Billows of glory swept over me until my joy seemed to be utterly inexpressible and uncontainable. Oh, the blessedness of that hour! Surely heaven could be no better. And from that day to the present—now almost twenty years—Satan has never had the audacity to tempt me to doubt even for one minute that God did not then and there sanctify me wholly.

In the spring of 1884 I accepted a position in a printing office in Indianapolis, Ind. After coming to this city God distinctly and unmistakably called me to preach His gospel. It would require another chapter to give all the details of the struggle through which I now passed, as for three months I prayed against this conviction. In view of my limited education, poverty, etc., I felt that it was utterly impossible for me to enter the ministry. However, I came to feel "Woe is me if I preach not the Gospel" and on a Monday afternoon about 3 o'clock, while on my knees, God seemed to speak to me direct in the words of Luke 21:15; "I will give you a mouth and wisdom, which all your adversaries shall not be able to gainsay nor resist." Those words had never before come to my notice. At the time, they seemed to have been spoken to me personally and audibly. This greatly assured and comforted my heart. The "open door" of opportunity in the providence of God, was at once before me. I selected as my first text, Matt. 11:28-30, and by the blessing of God, preached as best I could. While I was thus endeavoring to preach, sinners wept and saints shouted. I gave an invitation for any desiring to seek the Lord to come to the altar of prayer. Although there had been no revival in progress, five penitents came to the altar, and three were happily converted that night. Soon after this the call of God to the special work of holiness evangelism came to me just as clearly and certainly as had been my conversion, sanctification and call to preach. Again, in a most mysterious manner, the open door of opportunity was before me, and so in the fall of that same year (1884) I accepted an invitation to assist a church in a special series of revival meetings, and resigned my position in the printing office. Since that time I have never had a vacation of three weeks, and have averaged more than one sermon a day each year. I have preached and testified the gospel of holiness everywhere, and have never had a revival engagement, where the services continued one week or more without seekers at the altar. I regard it as a conservative statement when I say that in my meetings I have witnessed more than thirty thousand souls kneel at the altar seeking pardon or heart purity. Four times I was elected as Presiding Elder—each time over my protest—but with it continued the work of holiness evangelism. I have traveled more than one hundred and fifty thousand miles in filling my engagements, and have labored in thirty-three states and Canada, among twenty-five different denominations. Eighteen months of this time I have been associate pastor of the Church of the Nazarene in Los Angeles, Cal., but during all that time there never was a week without souls being saved and sanctified at our altars. To God be all the glory. Surely "by the grace of God I am what I am."

C. W. RUTH.

DEFINITIONS OF SANCTIFICATION.

Men speak of the subject of sanctification as though it were something so mysterious and incomprehensible that but very few could know its meaning. While its reality can only be known as the result of experience, the meaning of the word may be found by consulting almost any dictionary, just as one finds the meaning or definition of any other word. While different phases of the subject may be emphasized by different lexicographers there is a most substantial agreement regarding the fact of this word having both a human and a divine aspect; the human feature being a consecration and devotement to God and His service, and the divine work in sanctification a complete deliverance and purification from all sin. To use the word contradictory to these authenticated definitions is to do violence to the word and make words meaningless. No man is at liberty to say that light means darkness or darkness light.

WEBSTER'S DICTIONARY.

SANCTIFY.—"1. To make sacred or holy, to set apart to a holy or religious use, to consecrate by appropriate rites, to hallow. . . . 2. To make free from sin, to cleanse from moral corruption and pollution, to purify. John 17:17, Esp. (Theol.) the act of God's grace by which the affections of men are purified or alienated from sin and the world, and exalted to a supreme love to God." Surely this is language that can be understood and is all desirable.

CENTURY DICTIONARY.

SANCTIFY:—"To make holy or clean, either ceremonially or morally and spiritually; to purify or free from sin. . . . In Theology, the act of God's grace by which the affections of men are purified and the soul is cleansed from sin and consecrated to God . . . conformity of the heart and life to the will of God."

"The act of God's grace," hence it cannot be obtained by works or growth; a divine act; "cleansed from sin." Pardon and cleansing are not identical.

IMPERIAL DICTIONARY.

SANCTIFY:—"To make holy or sacred; to separate, set apart or appoint to a holy, sacred or religious use. 2. To purify in order to prepare for divine service and for partaking of holy things. 3. To purify from sin, to make holy."

"Set apart;" "to purify from sin" which is "to prepare for divine service." Should not all Christians desire and experience this preparation for service?

WORCESTER'S DICTIONARY.

SANCTIFY:—"1. To free from the power of sin; to cleanse from corruption; to make holy . . . sanctification; the act of sanctifying, or purifying from the dominion of sin. 2. The act of consecrating or setting apart to a sacred end or office; consecration."

"To free from the power of sin." Who would not desire deliverance from the power and dominion of sin?

UNIVERSAL DICTIONARY.

SANCTIFY:—"1. To make holy or sacred; to consecrate. 2. To make holy or godly; to purify from sin." "To make holy or godly." The word godly means God-like. How a person can love God, who is the essence and embodiment of holiness and then be averse or antagonistic to sanctification which is to make them holy and godly is indeed a mystery.

STANDARD DICTIONARY.

SANCTIFY:—"1. To make holy; rendered sacred: morally or spiritually pure, cleansed from sin . . . sanctification; specifically in Theology, the gracious work of the Holy Spirit whereby the believer is freed from sin and exalted to holiness of heart and life."

"Whereby the believer is freed from sin." According to this, sanctification is an experience for believers—not for sinners. This would make sanctification a second experience. "The gracious work of the Holy Spirit"—not of works, nor growth, nor death, nor purgatory, but a work of God divinely inwrought by the Holy Spirit. We can never grow into something God must do for us.

AMERICAN ENCYCLOPEDIA.

SANCTIFY:—"To make holy or sacred; to consecrate or set apart . . . to purify from sin . . . sanctification. Technically, an operation of the Spirit of God (Rom. 15:16; 2 Thess. 2:13; 1 Pet. 1:2) on those who are already in Jesus, i. e., are united to Him by faith (1 Cor. 1:2) by which they are rendered increasingly holy, dying to sin and living to God, to righteousness and to holiness, (Rom. 6:6, 11, 13, 19; 1 Thess. 5:23; 1 Pet. 2:24)."

Surely this is explicit enough. "An operation of the Spirit of God on those who are already in Jesus." An experience for "those who are already in Jesus." A second work, a divine work; consequently it must be obtained by faith; Acts 26:18.

Thus we see that there is an agreement, even as Adam Clark says in his commentary on John 17:17. "The word has two meanings: 1. It signifies to consecrate, to separate from earth and common use and to devote or dedicate to God and His service. 2. It signifies to make holy or pure. The prayer of Christ may be understood in both of these senses."

METHODIST EPISCOPAL CATECHISM.

"The act of Divine grace whereby we are made holy."

Not an experience to be reached by growth, but by an "act of Divine grace."

WESTMINSTER CONFESSION OF FAITH.

"They who are effectually called and regenerated having a new heart and a new spirit created in them, are further sanctified, really and personally, through the virtue of Christ's death and resurrection by His Word and His Spirit dwelling in them."

Here again it is recognized that sanctification is for such as "are effectually called and regenerated" and that it is accomplished "by His Word and His Spirit," and not by death or purgatory.

DEFINITIONS OF SANCTIFICATION. 19

JOHN WESLEY.

"Sanctification in the proper sense is an instantaneous deliverance from all sin, and includes an instantaneous power then given always to cleave to God."

"An instantaneous deliverance from all sin" and not a protracted and tedious process of growth. There is a gradual approach to the blessing, so far as the human part of consecration, preparation and faith is concerned, but the Divine work of "deliverance from all sin" is instantaneous.

POPE'S THEOLOGY.

Vol. 2, Page 64.

"Sanctification in its beginnings, process and final issues is the full eradication of the sin itself, which, reigning in the unregenerate co-exists with the new life in the regenerate, is abolished in the wholly sanctified."

Pope was a Wesleyan Theologian and is an accepted authority on Christian doctrine in Methodism. He declares there is a sin which "co-exists with the new life in the regenerate" which, however, "is abolished in the wholly sanctified."

REV. W. F. MALLALIEU.

Bishop in the M. E. Church.

"From the very first years of my ministry to the present time I have held with Adam Clark, Richard Watson, John Fletcher and John Wesley, that regeneration and entire sanctification are separate and distinct one from the other, and therefore received at different times—both received by faith and the last one the privilege of every believer as the first is of every penitent." To all this we say, Amen and amen.

MATTHEW HENRY'S COMMENTARY.

"It is the prayer of Christ for all that are His, that they may be sanctified."

SAMUEL RUTHERFORD.

the saintly Scottish Presbyterian divine said, "Christ is more to be loved for giving us sanctification than justification. It is in some respects greater love in Him to sanctify than to justify, for He maketh us like himself in His own essential portraiture and image in sanctification."

The words "sanctify" and sanctification" are made from the Latin adjective *sanctus* (meaning "holy") and the Latin verb *facere* (meaning "to make") and the suffix *"tion"* always meaning "the act of." So the root meaning of the word, plainly means and signifies the act of making holy. Many more splendid authorities might be adduced, but these definitions from so many well known and accepted standards should suffice to convince any Christian of his privilege and high calling in the Gospel.

"Christ also loved the Church, and gave Himself for it; that He might sanctify and cleanse it." Eph. 5:25-26. "Wherefore Jesus also, that He might sanctify the people with His own blood, suffered without the gate. Let us go forth therefore unto Him without the Camp, bearing His reproach." Heb. 13:12-13.

SIX THEORIES OF SANCTIFICATION.

No man can make an honest pretense to believing the Bible, and not believe in some sort of sanctification. According to Cruden's concordance, the words "sanctify," "sanctified" and "sanctification" may be found at least one hundred and sixty-four times in the Bible. So when one declares he does not believe in sanctification, he simply exposes either his ignorance or his infidelity concerning the Bible. In order to believe the Bible, we are bound to believe in some sort of sanctification. Practically, there are but six theories regarding this experience.

FIRST THEORY.

The first theory is that justification and sanctification are experienced simultaneously; that whoever is justified is also sanctified. Those holding this theory may be heard to say they "got all when they were converted." But this theory is contrary to the Scripture and universal experience. Every command, exhortation, prayer, and promise in the Bible touching the subject of sanctification is for Christians—never for sinners. If Christians are sanctified when justified, why should sanctification be subsequently enjoined upon them? In writing to the Corinthian church, (1 Cor. 3:1-3) the Apostle addressed them as "brethren," said they were "babes in Christ," and declared he had fed them "with milk." A "babe *in* Christ" is just as certainly *in* Christ as an adult in Christ; there must have been a spiritual birth—a spiritual being—or they could not have received spiritual food and nourishment. But in verse three he says, plainly, "Ye are yet carnal," which undeniably is evidence that they were not yet wholly sanctified, though they were "in Christ." In the first chapter and fourth verse, he said, "I thank my God always on your behalf, for the grace of God which is given you by Jesus Christ." According to this they had "the grace of God given them by Jesus Christ;" more, they had such measure of grace given them that the Apostle found it an occasion for continuous thanksgiving. Still he declares they were "yet carnal." Who ever heard a minister inviting a sinner to seek sanctification? Not only is this theory contrary to all Scripture, but contrary to all human experience. Every truly converted soul has felt the motions and stirrings of carnality in his heart subsequent to pardon, manifesting itself in fear, anger, unbelief, pride, selfwill, despondency, etc., etc. We venture the assertion that no young convert has ever gone six months from the place of his conversion without finding some of these things in his heart, which is in evidence that the roots of carnality were still within. Again, no young convert has ever thought of testifying to sanctification as an experience unless in a second blessing meeting. If space would permit we could show that the Apostles were not sanctified when they were justified, nor the Ephesians, nor the Galatians, nor the Romans, nor the Samaritans, nor the Colossians, nor Abraham, nor David, nor Isaiah, etc., but that all these obtained it as a second experience.

SECOND THEORY.

The second theory is that sanctification is attained by a growth in grace. This theory is an absurdity for the reason that we can never grow impurity out of the heart.

If sanctification were by growth, then time is a factor, for all will admit that it requires time to grow; if time is a factor, then we may well raise the question, "How much time is required?" "How long must we grow in grace before we are wholly sanctified?" Suppose one might be said to grow into sanctification in two years; (which would be a very short time as compared with many who have been known to be growing in grace for the space of forty years and have not yet reached it) and now suppose that individual should die at the expiration of one year, when it might be said he has come by the process of growth, just half way to sanctification, what about the matter? Would not the last half of sanctification, of necessity, have to take place instantly? And if the last half of sanctification might be completed instantly, why not the first half? To hope for sanctification by growth is hoping in a theory that can never be realized. Sanctification is plainly a "divine act," obtained instantaneously by an entire consecration and faith. As well speak of growing into justification as growing into sanctification; as in the former, so in the latter; it is something Jesus must do for us. "Wherefore Jesus also, that He might sanctify the people with His own blood, suffered without the gate." Heb. 13-12.

THIRD THEORY.

The third theory is that "sanctification takes place in death; that no one can be sanctified in this life." We answer death has no saving efficacy. If death could deliver a Christian from some sin, why might it not deliver a sinner from all sin? Then there would be no need of a Savior or of the cleansing blood, and death would be a savior. Satan is the direct cause of sin and sin is the cause of death; this would make death Satan's grand-child. One could hardly hope for deliverance from sin from this source. While doubtless some persons have received the grace of sanctification on their death-bed, it was evidently by the cleansing blood of Jesus and not by death. If the blood of Jesus can cleanse us from all sin when dying, why might it not cleanse us from all sin while in life? Has the blood of Jesus more cleansing power when a man is dying than when he is living? Certainly not. Not a single passage of scripture can be cited that gives us promise of salvation or cleansing at the time of dissolution. The Epistle of Jude was written "To them that are sanctified" (Jude 1:1). If they were not sanctified until death, this epistle must have been written to them after they were dead, for it was written after they were sanctified. But this verse says, they were "sanctified by God the Father;" not by death.

FOURTH THEORY.

The fourth theory is that sanctification is a sort of post-mortem affair, and takes place after death, in Purgatory. While the priest may absolve the sinner from his guilt, it is necessary that he should nevertheless pass through Purgatorial fires in order to be thoroughly refined and freed from sin. But we insist that this is sheer nonsense—that the Bible makes no mention of a Purgatory, but rather teaches that as death leaves us the Judgment will find us. It has been observed that even they who advocate this theory seem to believe that the time their dupes should spend in Purgatory might be determined by the size of the purse of the deceased. If they or their friends have plenty money the priest will engage to pray them out speedily; but where the necessary fee is not forthcoming, the deceased are left to sweat it through Purgatory as best they may. How any sensible person could accept such a delusion is indeed a mystery. Since Jesus has given definite promise concerning "every branch that beareth fruit, He purgeth it," (John 15:2) I prefer to trust Him for the purging, rather than humanly invented purgatorial fires.

FIFTH THEORY.

The fifth theory is the Calvinistic, Keswickian Antinomian theory of *repression* and *imputed* holiness as opposed to the Wesleyan theory of *eradication* of inbred sin and *imparted* holiness. Says one of their writers, "He who is our Great High Priest before God is pure, without sin. God sees Him as such, and He stands for us who are His people, and we are accepted in Him. His holiness is ours by imputation. Standing in Him we are in the sight of God, holy as Christ is holy, and pure as Christ is pure. God looks at our representative, and He sees us in Him. We are complete in Him who is our spotless and glorious Head." According to this theory the individual in reality can never become holy; that while he within himself is not holy, Christ's holiness is imputed to him, and for His sake the individual is accounted holy. This theory clearly makes void such passages as I John 1:7, "The blood of Jesus Christ His Son cleanseth us from all sin"; or Rom. 6:22, "But now being made free from sin," etc. According to this theory Satan has despoiled the holiness and image of God in man and Christ cannot restore it. What folly. "Blessed are the pure in heart, for they shall see God."

THE SIXTH THEORY.

The sixth theory is, that sanctification is an experience subsequent to regeneration, conditioned upon entire consecration and faith, the privilege of every believer, to be experienced and enjoyed in this life. That by the baptism with the Holy Ghost inbred sin is destroyed and the heart perfected in love. The people holding this theory are the only people who, personally, have any experience or testimony to sanctification. These believe that sin has never gone so deep into the soul, but that the blood of Jesus can go deeper. "That where sin abounded grace did much more abound." Jesus believed sanctification a divine act, for He prayed the Father to sanctify the disciples, John 17:17. Indeed, the Trinity enters into our sanctification. God the Father wills our sanctification, I Thess. 4:3. In order to provide our sanctification Jesus suffered without the gate, Heb. 13:12. And the Holy Ghost witnesses to our sanctification, Heb. 10:14, 15. It is said of Bible saints, they were "sanctified by God the Father," Jude 1:1; also that Jesus sanctifies, Eph. 5:25-27; and of the offering up of the Gentiles it was said they were "sanctified by the Holy Ghost." Rom. 15:16. In Acts 26:18 we find that sanctification is obtained by faith. Seeing it is a work that God must do for us, we need not wait for growth, death or purgatory, but may by faith enter this blessed experience the instant the consecration is entire and complete. While there is a gradual approach to the experience from the human side, the divine work is instantaneous. Hallelujah!

SANCTIFICATION AND ENTIRE SANCTIFICATION.

These terms, as relating to personal experience, are frequently used interchangeably, as though they were synonymous, although, critically speaking, they are not the same. Many of the early writers, as did Mr. Wesley, clearly distinguished between sanctification and *entire* sanctification, or the being *wholly* sanctified. To see the propriety and scripturalness of this distinction one need only bear in mind the two-fold definition of the word sanctification, given and acknowledged by all our dictionaries and commentaries, as may perhaps best be stated in the language of Adam Clark, in commenting on the prayer of Jesus, "Sanctify them through thy truth; thy word is truth." He says, 'This word has two meanings: 1. It signifies to consecrate, to separate from earthly and common use and to devote or dedicate to God and His service. 2. It signifies to make holy or pure. The prayer of Christ may be understood in both these senses." To these two definitions there is a substantial agreement. And men do this subject gross injustice, and convict themselves either of great ignorance, or of wilful deceit, when they insist that sanctification refers exclusively to a "setting apart to God and his service."

As stated above, "Sanctify" does mean, "to consecrate, to separate," "to devote or dedicate," "but it also signifies "to make holy or pure." According to Webster's Dictionary it means, 2. "To cleanse from moral corruption and pollution, to purify. John 17:17. Esp. (Theol.) the act of God's grace by which the affections of men are purified or alienated from sin and the world, and exalted to a supreme love to God." Passing strange it is that multitudes never seem to recognize this latter definition.

Having this two-fold definition clearly in mind, it may be easily understood how there is a difference in being sanctified in part, and being sanctified entirely or wholly. So far as the human side of sanctification is concerned, namely, that of "consecration," "separation," "dedication" or "devotement," it may be said, just in so far as the individual has thus "consecrated," "separated." "dedicated" and "devoted" himself to God, for the purpose of being thus purified and made holy, thus far he has sanctified himself. However, it is well to remember that this consecration, separation, dedication and devotement is to God, and not to any particular work or calling, as is frequently done; and that this consecration must have as its objective point the purifying and cleansing of the heart from all sin, before it can be regarded as any part of entire sanctification. While in the wilderness, the children of Israel doubtless frequently left their tents, for various reasons other than that of crossing the Jordan, and therefore this leaving of their tents could not be regarded as any part of the necessary steps for reaching the promised land. But on a certain day it was said, with the distinct object of crossing Jordan into Canaan, "Sanctify ourselves." "and it came to pass, when the people removed from their tents *to pass over Jordan,*" "that the waters which came down from above stood and rose up upon an heap," &c. It was only when they sanctified themselves and "removed from their tents" for the express purpose of crossing *"over Jordan,"* that removing from their tents could be regarded as any part of the steps necessary to entering Canaan. Hence, a person may be consecrated, separated, devoted and dedicated to a work, or to God, for the performance of that certain work, and yet such consecration or devotement could not be regarded as any part of entire sanctification, as the consecration thus made does not contemplate the individual's entire sanctification, and is made for an entirely different purpose.

And in this connection it is well to note that this human side of sanctification,—which is but the approach to, and the condition of *entire* sanctification—may be gradual. That is, the individual may be sometime in entirely completing this "separation'," "dedication" and "devotement" of his all to God. But the moment this human side of sanctification is completed, and every condition met, faith in reality touching the promise, the divine side of sanctification, which is "to make holy or pure;" to make free from sin, to cleanse from moral corruption and pollution, to purify," is instantaneously and divinely inwrought by the application of the virtue of the atonement through the power of the Holy Ghost. In the language of Adam Clark: "Neither the *gradatim* pardon nor the *seriatim* purification exists in the Bible." Mr. Wesley said, "To talk of this work (entire sanctification) as being gradual, would be nonsense, as much as if we talked of gradual justification." "As to the manner, I believe this perfection is *always* wrought in the soul by a simple act of faith; consequently in an instant."

In justice to those who differ with us, it is proper that we say, Mr. Wesley did recognize this two-fold definition of sanctification, and so taught that "at the same time that we are justified, yea, at that very moment sanctification begins (*Idem*, p. 237) "From the time of our being born again, the gradual work of sanctification takes place." (*Idem*, p. 238). But to infer that by this he taught or believed that the divine side of sanctification, the making "holy or pure," "to make free from sin"—was gradual is to make Mr. Wesley contradict himself. In his Journal, under date of May 21, 1761, Mr. Wesley wrote of those who had sought sanctification by works, and "thought it was to come gradually," "What wonder is it, then, that you have been fighting all these years as one that beateth the air?"

To teach that the divine work of sanctification in the purifying and cleansing of the heart from all sin is a gradual work would be to admit that a heart might be a little holy, more holy and most holy, so that it might become exceedingly difficult to know just in what degree of holiness the individual experience might be located. And how to pronounce a heart holy that had yet any trace of sin in it, would be another difficulty; and then in case death should overtake the individual before he had reached the third degree of holiness, where he might be said to be most holy, there might be another embarrassing difficulty, seeing that holiness—freedom from all sin—is the only condition or fitness for seeing God.

"The very God of peace sanctify you wholly; and I pray

God your whole spirit, and soul, and body be preserved blameless unto the coming of our Lord Jesus Christ. Faithful is He that calleth you who also will do it." 1 Thes. 5:23, 24. Thank God, the promise of cleansing from "all sin" is in the present tense. "If we walk in the light as He is in the light, we have fellowship one with another, and the blood of Jesus Christ His Son cleanseth us from all sin." 1 Jno. 1:7. The human side of sanctification may be partial or gradual, but entire sanctification in which the heart is cleansed from all sin, is always instantaneous and complete.

DISTINCTIONS BETWEEN JUSTIFICATION AND SANCTIFICATION.

(The terms Justification and Sanctification are not used in a technical or critical sense, but rather in a general sense as referring to experience.)

In Justification there is life.
In Sanctification there is life more abundant.

In Justification there is love.
In Sanctification there is perfect love which casteth out fear.

In Justification the "old man" is repressed.
In Sanctification the "old man" is destroyed.

In Justification there is "peace with God."
In Sanctification there is "the peace of God."

Justification gives us a right to heaven.
Sanctification gives the fitness for heaven.

In Justification we "put on the new man."
In Sanctification we "put off the old man with his deeds"

In Justification there is joy—intermittent joy.
In Sanctification there is fullness of joy—abiding joy.

Justification includes pardon, which is a judicial act.
Sanctification includes a cleansing, which is a priestly function.

Justification is obtained by surrender, repentance and faith.
Sanctification is obtained by obedience, consecration and faith.

Justification delivers from guilt and condemnation.
Sanctification delivers from unholy tempers and abnormal appetites.

In Justification the Holy Spirit is with the believer.
In Sanctification the Holy Spirit is in the believer. (John 14:17.)

Justification comprehends adoption; making us children of God.
Sanctification comprehends anointing, making us kings and priests unto God.

Justification separates us from the world, so we are no longer of the world.
Sanctification takes the world out of us; worldly desires and ambitions.

Justification is illustrated by the rescue of the sinking man from the water.
Sanctification is getting the water out of the lungs of the drowning man.

Justification is conditioned on confession of sin. (1 John 1:9.)
Sanctification is conditioned on walking "in the light as He is in the light." (1 John 1:7.)

Justification has to do with sin as an act—sins committed.
Sanctification has to do with sin as a principle—the sin nature we inherited.

Justification comes by the birth of the Spirit—when the repentant sinner is born again.
Sanctification comes by the baptism with the Spirit—when the believer has a personal pentecost.

Justification restores to us the favor of God which we had lost through our own disobedience.
Sanctification restores to us holiness or the moral likeness of God, which we had lost through Adam's disobedience.

Justification is the impartation of a spiritual nature, bringing us into possession of eternal life.
Sanctification is the crucifixion and destruction of our carnal nature, making us dead indeed unto sin.

Justification destroys the "shoots" of sin.
Sanctification destroys the "roots" of sin.

Justification makes us free—free from outward sin and condemnation.

Sanctification makes "free indeed." Gives the "deed" to our freedom with all the mortgages paid off. Freedom from fear, and doubt, and pride, etc.

In Justification we are united to Christ as the branch to the vine.

In Sanctification we receive the purging promised to the living, fruitful vine, that we may "bring forth more fruit." (John 15:2.)

In Justification the experience is a "well of water," (John 4:14). A well is for personal use.

In Sanctification there is a fullness of blessing so that out of our inward parts "shall flow rivers of living water." (John 6:38-39). A river cannot be confined to personal use, but will bless and fructify wherever it flows.

JUSTIFICATION: "The forensic, judicial or gracious act of God by which *the sinner* is declared righteous, or justly free from the obligation to penalty and fully restored to divine favor."—*Standard Dictionary.*

SANCTIFICATION: "To make holy; cleanse from sin. Specifically in theology, the gracious work of the Holy Spirit whereby *the believer* is freed from sin, and exalted to holiness of heart and life."—*Standard Dictionary.*

JUSTIFICATION NOT A HALF WAY WORK.

It is urged by those who are averse to the "second blessing" that in order to make place for a second experience the holiness people are under the necessity of minifying and depreciating the work of justification.

There is no occasion to minify justification, and the facts are, no one more fully appreciates and magnifies the work of justification than sanctified people. Instead of saying that justification is but a half-way work, they believe that justification comprehends at least ten perfect works, viz.:

1. *Conviction.* The Holy Spirit alone can fully awaken and convict the world "of sin and of righteousness and of judgment." Genuine Holy Ghost conviction must precede repentance; conviction for sin is within itself a perfect work.

2. *Surrender.* There must be a complete yielding—an unconditional surrender to God. God will never save a man who insists on dictating terms. The mental reservation of one sin, or hesitation to comply with one condition, will mean darkness, condemnation and loss of the soul. The surrender must be complete and entire.

3. *Repentance.* Repentance toward God is indispensable to Bible salvation. The lack of genuine repentance accounts for much of the superficiality of religion in these days. Repentance comprehends at least five distinct things, to wit: A consciousness of sin and guilt; a deep heart sorrow for sin; the confession of sin; restitution; and the abandonment of sin. Repentance is within itself a perfect work.

4. *Pardon.* When there is genuine repentance God grants a full and free pardon. Not half our sins, but every sin ever committed is fully pardoned, never to be remembered against us. This takes place in the thought of God, and is something done for us. The pardon of sins is a perfect work within itself.

5. *Regeneration.* The quickening of the soul into newness of life; the impartation of divine, spiritual and eternal life. The soul regenerated by the Holy Spirit is not made partially alive, but fully alive, so that it can be said, "We know that we have passed from death unto life."

6. *Washing of Regeneration.* Sin defiles and pollutes. Hence men not only need pardon, but washing and cleansing from this acquired pollution resulting from their sins. This is termed "the washing of regeneration," and includes that work of the Spirit in which He did "purge your conscience from dead works." This, too, is a gracious and complete work.

7. *Adoption.* The person fully pardoned is now adopted into the family of God; not partially adopted, but fully adopted, and "the Spirit of adoption" given in his heart, whereby he cries, "Abba, Father." His name is written in heaven, and he becomes a son of God—an heir of God and a joint heir with Christ. Adoption is within itself another perfect work.

8. *Witness of the Spirit.* "The Spirit itself beareth witness with our spirit that we are the children of God." When the soul finds acceptance with God there is the divine attestation—the witness of the Spirit to the inner con-

sciousness, giving knowledge and assurance, so there can be no doubt or uncertainty as to the question of our acceptance with God; a telegram from the skies, a certificate signed in heaven—the voice of God in the soul, bringing confidence, gladness and assurance forever. These latter five usually occur simultaneously.

9. *Power.* "As many as received Him, to them gave He power to become the sons of God." This is power to resist temptation and do the will of God. The second-blessing people are about the only people who really believe and teach that "whosoever is born of God doth not commit sin." They insist that justification will save men from sinning; in so saying they magnify the work of justification, while they who insist on a "sinning religion" greatly minify justification. A justification that saves from sinning is a perfect work.

10. *Faith.* "Without faith it is impossible to please Him." The exercise of a perfect faith, appropriating and resting upon the word of God, is one of the conditions of light and life in the soul. "He that believeth not shall be damned." "Therefore, being justified by faith we have peace with God, through our Lord Jesus Christ."

All persons truly justified have experienced these ten points. But all this has to do with sins committed, and is only preparatory to sanctification. Sanctification deals with altogether a different problem, namely, *inherited sin*—the crucifixion of "our old man." Justification is the foundation upon which rests the superstructure of sanctification. Justification is an excellent experience, but sanctification is a "more excellent" experience.

SANCTIFICATION A SECOND BLESSING.

"CHRIST also loved *the Church* and gave Himself for *it;* that He might sanctify and cleanse *it.*" Sanctification was never provided for nor promised to the world, but to the Church; *the Church* is not made of sinners, but of true believers who have been born again.

Mr. John Wesley, in writing to Miss Jane Hilton, in 1774, said, "It is exceedingly certain that God did give you the *second blessing,* properly so called. He delivered you from the root of bitterness, from inbred as well as actual sin." (Vol. 8, p. 45.) He used the same phrase with reference to sanctification on other occasions. Mr. Charles Wesley called it "that *second rest.*" Martin Luther referred to it as a "second conversion;" Andrew Murray has referred to this grace as a "second crisis." Paul, in writing to the Church at Corinth, spoke of a "second benefit," or as the margin gives it, "a second grace." (2. Cor. 1:15.

But why call it a "second blessing"? Because such it is. We have frequently heard the objector say, sneeringly: "I have not only received the '*second* blessing,' but I have received hundreds of blessings." And yet, strange to say, this same person was averse to the preaching of a "second blessing" and became offended when other people sought and professed the same. A man who could lay claim to a hundred blessings certainly should not object to those who insist on having at least a "second blessing." The facts are, a man may have a hundred blessings and not have "the second blessing, properly so called." Indeed a *sinner* might boast of a hundred blessings, and still be without hope—a lost soul. Life, health, food, Christian parentage, an open Bible, church privileges, conviction, etc., etc., should all be counted as blessings.

Sanctification is the "second blessing" exactly in the same sense that justification is the *first* blessing. Justification is the first blessing that changes our moral condition and our personal relation toward God. In justification we are changed from the attitude and relation of enemies and rebels toward God into that of obedient children. It certainly is a blessing—but it is more, it is a grace that transforms and transposes into a permanent state and experience. Until this experience, all other blessings left the individual in the same moral condition they had found him. So, after a person is fully justified, he may receive not only many temporal, but many spiritual blessings—prayer meeting and campmeeting blessings—which will greatly refresh, and help, and encourage, and yet they will not eradicate inbred sin, and make him holy; if he was given to fear or impatience or doubt, or any other carnal manifestations, those same conditions will continue to exist after the "hundreds of blessings" have come and gone.

Exactly as justification is the first blessing that effects a permanent inward change, so sanctification is the "second blessing," hence, "properly so called." While justification comprehends pardon, regeneration and adoption, making us children of God, sanctification comprehends the full eradication of the carnal mind, the inbred sin, and the baptism and anointing with the Holy Ghost, making us kings and priests unto God. Whereas justification delivers us from sins committed, sin as an act, sanctification delivers us from the sin-nature inherited—sin as a principle; justification delivers us from guilt and condemnation while sanctification delivers us from unholy appetites; the first gives us the birth of the Spirit; the second, the baptism with the Spirit. Just as certainly as justification marks a distinct epoch and crisis in the life of those receiving it, just so certainly sanctification marks a second epoch, a second crisis, a second experience, and therefore is a "second blessing, properly so called."

Again, it is urged that the term *"second blessing"* is not in the Bible and therefore must not be used. While we admit that this exact phrase is not in the Bible, we do insist that the equivalent, that which can mean nothing else, is in the Bible. Such it is in every case where sanctification, holiness, perfection, etc., is urged upon the church—which is made up of those who are already "in Christ." Who would think of objecting to the terms, *"the new birth," "salvation from sin," "a child of God,"* etc, and yet these exact phrases cannot be found in the Bible; however, we have their equivalent over and over and therefore these terms are perfectly proper. Seeing that sanctification is a "second blessing, properly so called" there can be no reasonable objection to the use of the term.

THAT "SOMETHING."

"I knew Jesus and He was precious to my soul; but I found *something* within that would not be sweet, and patient and kind; I did what I could to keep it down, but it was there; I besought Jesus to do something for me, and when I gave Him my will He came in, and took out all that would not be sweet and patient and kind, and then He shut the door." Thus testified George Fox, the founder of the Society of Friends, more than two centuries ago. After he "knew Jesus" there was still *"something within"* which was antagonistic to the spiritual life implanted; nor was this experience peculiar to him alone. Such is indeed the experience of every new born and truly regenerated soul. While they may not understand the subject of entire sanctification, and perhaps never have heard of the "second blessing," yet, a young convert seldom goes three months in the new found experience, until he becomes painfully conscious that there remains a "something within" that hinders, and retards his spiritual progress, and often becomes a source of much distress.

The manifestations of that "something" vary, but frequently the first showing of it is in a man-fearing spirit, or anger, or a disposition to doubt, or an unforgiving spirit, etc. Then comes frequently the temptation, that perhaps, after all there had not been a true conversion or these things would not manifest themselves, and because they had not been properly instructed, many have wearied of the conflict and struggle and have cast away their confidence.

The Bible name for that "something" is, "the carnal mind" which, "is enmity against God: for it is not subject to the law of God, neither indeed can be" Rom. 8:7. Paul said of the Corinthians, "I thank my God always on your behalf, for the grace of God which is given you by Jesus Christ," and said, because they were "babes in Christ," "I have fed you with milk," "ye are yet carnal", thus showing that the carnal mind is not eradicated in conversion, but still continues in those who are "in Christ for a "babe in Christ" is just as certainly "in Christ" as an adult in Christ is in Christ.

Then again the Bible speaks of that *"something"* as "the flesh;" "The flesh lusteth against the Spirit, and the Spirit against the flesh and these are contrary the one to the other, so that ye cannot do the things that ye would." Gal. 5:17. Here the dual nature is clearly set forth, and the inward conflict indicated. While the man has "the Spirit" (which would not apply to a sinner) he also has a something antagonistic to the Spirit, called here "the flesh." But in verse 24, we read, "And they that are Christ's have crucified the flesh," showing that the divine process for that "something" is not pardon, nor suppression, but crucifixion, which signifies that there is something to die and thus to be destroyed.

Other names given in the Bible for that "something" is, "sin that dwelleth in me," "the law of sin" "the body of this death" "the sin which doth so easily beset" "the sin of the world" "the body of sin", "our old man" etc., all of which have reference to that "something within" remaining after we are converted; in common parlance it is called "inbred sin", "depravity" "our evil nature" "original sin" our "Adamic nature," etc. All of these terms are synonymous, and refer to this identical "something within" which is the common heritage of every child of Adam. God's method and purpose is to "crucify" and "destroy" that something—"our old man"—so that we are "dead indeed unto sin." The sins committed may be pardoned, but this "something" can not be pardoned for the simple reason we did not commit the same; it was born in us, and as the Anglican Confession says, "This infection of nature doth remain, yea, even in them that have been regenerated." But thank God, there is power in Jesus' blood to eliminate and destroy it. "Knowing this, that our old man is crucified with him, that the body of sin might be destroyed, that henceforth we should not serve sin." Rom. 6:6. This deliverance is what Mr. Wesley termed "the second blessing properly so called." This is sanctification, and is the privilege of every believer, as pardon is the privilege of every penitent sinner.

ESSENTIALS TO SANCTIFICATION.

1. JUSTIFICATION.

A clear-cut, definite experience in pardon and regeneration. While there is a lingering doubt about your acceptance with God—any back account, or "unfinished business"—the soul cannot exercise intelligent faith for sanctification. Sanctification is no where in the Bible proffered to sinners, nor to backsliders, but in every instance to justified believers. "Christ also loved *the Church,* and gave Himself for it; that He might sanctify and cleanse it." Eph. 5:25, 26. A sinner or backslider does not belong to *"the Church,"* and therefore is not eligible to sanctification.

2. DEFINITE SEEKING.

A sinner may pray for pardon in an indefinite, roundabout way for forty years and never obtain pardon. But when he definitely repents and seeks God with all his heart he soon finds Him in the pardon of sin. Exactly so a Christian may pray and seek for a "higher life," a "deeper work of grace," "more religion," or to get "nearer to Jesus," etc., etc., for forty years and never get sanctified. But when a person seeks definitely to be sanctified wholly, and desperately and persistently strikes out across lots to find sanctification, such a soul will speedily and surely obtain this great experience.

3. PERFECT OBEDIENCE.

It is positively necessary that the soul welcome and walk in all the light that God has given. Jesus had said to the disciples, "Tarry ye in the City of Jerusalem." Suppose they had said "Jerusalem is in an uproar, the mob that has crucified our Lord is still there, and our own lives would be greatly in peril in Jerusalem, therefore we will go out to Bethany, or up to Jericho, or some other place and "tarry" where there is no danger of our being disturbed or molested;" this might have been regarded as good reasoning and sound logic for the worldly wise, but would have been direct disobedience and would have forfeited to them the promise, and defeated the whole purpose of God. No use asking God for more light unless we are willing to walk in all the light He has given. A little brass jewelry, or a plug of tobacco, or some worldly association, or some questionable indulgence, etc., will keep a soul out of the blessing of sanctification after the call of God has come to abandon the same. The disobedient child cannot approach the parent with confidence. "If our heart condemn us not, then have we confidence toward God."

4. ENTIRE CONSECRATION.

Consecration is not the surrender of something evil,

but the offering up to God, unconditionally that which is good. The soul must be able to say, in the language of the poet:

> "Here I give my all to Thee,
> Friends, and time, and earthly store,
> Soul and body, Thine to be—
> Wholly Thine for evermore."

Entire consecration means the giving of all to God—all we have and all we expect to have; all we are and all we hope to be; all we know and all we do not know, with the promise of an eternal "yes" to all the will of God for all the future. It is not consecration to a work, or consecration to a certain calling, but consecration to God. It is not simply a desire to consecrate, or a willingness to consecrate but the unconditional and irrevocable signing of the deed of all to God for time and eternity.

5. FAITH.

"Without faith it is impossible to please Him." First there must be faith that there is such an experience; then there must be faith that this experience is provided for me, and that by meeting the conditions I can obtain it; then we need appropriating faith which lays hold on the promise and believes God does just now sanctify me because He said so. It is not sufficient to believe that He can, or that He will sanctify, but I must believe that He does just now sanctify me because I have met the conditions, and He does His part according to His promise. "Sanctified by faith." Acts 26:18. Amen.

SANCTIFICATION INCLUDES SEPARATION AND CONSECRATION.

Separation is not consecration and consecration is not sanctification; the one is the antecedent of the other. We have known a people who greatly emphasized the importance of separation from the world who nevertheless were not consecrated to God; in like manner we have known a people who have laid much stress upon consecration who did not believe in sanctification.

The importance of separation from the world can scarcely be exaggerated—especially so in view of the worldliness that has crept into the churches. God is still saying, "Be ye not unequally yoked together with unbelievers; for what fellowship hath righteousness with unrighteousness? and what communion hath light with darkness * * * wherefore come out from among them, and be ye separate, saith the Lord, and touch not the unclean thing: and I will receive you." (2 Cor. 6:14-17.) "Love not the world, neither the things that are in the world. *If any man love the world the love of the Father is not in him.*" (1 Jno. 2:15); "Know ye not that the friendship of the world is enmity with God? whosoever therefore will be a friend of the world is the enemy of God." (Jas. 4:4)

Surely these passages are sufficiently plain for all to understand. How men and women can court and intermarry with the world, be yoked up with all sorts of godless secret orders and worldly fraternities, follow all the fashions of dress and worldly attire, adorning themselves by the "wearing of gold" and "putting on of apparel" which is positively forbidden by the Word of God, and yet claim to be followers of Christ, and in some instances even profess sanctification, is indeed a mystery. "No man can serve two masters." "Be not conformed to this world, but be ye transformed by the renewing of your mind."

Being separated from the world we should now consecrate ourselves unconditionally to God for time and eternity, to be at His disposal for any service. When such a consecration is once made there can be no re-consecration. Re-consecration implies that something has been taken back, and therefore would necessitate repentance. It is not consecration to a work, but consecration to God, and then the person will be ready for any work in which God may be pleased to use him. Consecration is the presentation of ourselves and our all to God for sacrifice or service,—*"a living sacrifice,"* and is the pledge of an eternal "yes" to all the will of God, henceforth and forevermore.

Consecration is the condition of and preparation for sanctification. But while a person may declare his all on the altar, it requires a step of faith in which the provisions and promises of God for the cleansing from all sin are appropriated. Having done our part in making the consecration entire, it now remains for us to believe that God accepts and sanctifies the gift. However it is perfectly easy and natural for us to believe that God does His part when once we reach the confidence and assurance that we have paid the price of an unconditional, irrevocable and eternal abandonment of our all to Him. "For whether is greater the gift, or the altar that sanctifieth the gift." (Matt. 23:19.)

WHY NOT SANCTIFIED WHEN CONVERTED?

1. Because it is contrary to the word of God. God could do many things He does not do, simply because it is not His method or plan of doing. He could make twenty dollar gold pieces grow on sycamore trees if it were simply a question of power; but such is not His way of doing. So He unquestionably could sanctify a man wholly at the same instant He pardons his sins, but this is not His method as revealed in His word. He has never called or commanded a sinner to become sanctified, nor has He given any promises of sanctification to a sinner. In every instance where the command or promise of sanctification is given in the word of God it is to those who are already His people. In the study of God's word many cases can be pointed out where sanctification was not accomplished in conversion. God has method and system in all His works. What He does for one man in conversion He does for others; He does not have a half dozen ways of converting folks. The manifestations of that work may vary, but the same work is divinely inwrought.

2. The sinner does not realize his need of sanctification. The one thing that engages the attention of the penitent sinner is his guilt and condemnation, and the consequent results of his sins, and how he may find deliverance and obtain the favor of God. Had God sanctified me when He converted me He would have done so without my having understood my need or privilege of the same and without my asking. No sinner feels his need of sanctification, nor thinks of praying God to sanctify him when under conviction for sin and seeking pardon. And although there are preachers who insist that

justification and sanctification are simultaneous, not one would invite a penitent sinner to come and seek sanctification. If this is what a sinner should seek and expect to receive why should he not be told of it? After peace has been obtained, and the soul has the consciousness of pardon, and comes to see and feel its need of deliverance from "the sin which doth so easily beset," and understands that such is the will of God and the "inheritance among them which are sanctified by faith," there can be intelligent asking and compliance with conditions and proper appreciation of the gift bestowed.

3. The work of justification and the work of sanctification deal with two different phases of sin; the former having to do with sins committed—sin as an act, while sanctification has to do with sin inherited—sin as a principle or nature. In some particulars these works of the Spirit are antipodal—direct opposites. In justification there is the quickening of our moral natures—the impartation of a new life; in sanctification there is the destruction, and crucifixion—the deadening of our carnal nature "(our old man)" as in Rom. 6:6. The first a making alive process; the second a deadening process. Pardon and crucifixion are surely not identical. Our sins are never said to be crucified, nor "our old man" pardoned. This could not be so in the nature of the case. On the contrary, sins committed are pardoned, Isa. 55:7, and "our old man is crucified," Rom. 6:6. The first gives us the favor of God; the second restores to us the moral likeness and image of God; the first gives us a right to heaven; the second gives us the fitness for heaven. In the first we are born of the Spirit; in the second we

are baptized with the Spirit. In the nature of things a *birth* must precede a baptism. Just as certain as the birth of the Spirit marks a distinct crisis or epoch, just so certainly does the baptism with the Spirit mark the entrance upon a new era and life experience.

ERADICATION OR REPRESSION, WHICH?

THE facts of *"original sin"* are admitted by all Evangelical denominations. There is scarcely a denomination that does not make some reference to the subject of original sin in its creed, in some form or other, and so, clearly distinguishes between it—the sin-nature inherited—and sin as an act committed. That all men are born into this world with this "Adamic taint," this "infection of nature," this "inbred sin;" or, as it is termed in the Scripture, the "carnal mind," "our old man," "the body of sin," "sin that dwelleth in me," "the sin which doth so easily beset," &c., is generally recognized and conceded.

Nor is there any controversy touching the fact that this thing—termed "original sin"—cannot enter heaven, and therefore must be eradicated from the soul before there is perfect fitness for a holy heaven. The points of controversy are concerning the time and method for the accomplishment of this deliverance; the Calvinistic, Zinzendorfian, Keswickian theory being that this full deliverance cannot be fully realized until death; hence the only hope for the Christian in this life is to obtain grace to repress, subdue, regulate, control and overcome this evil within until death shall set us free. The Arminian, Wesleyan and present-day second-blessing, holiness-movement theory is, that subsequent to regeneration, by a complete consecration and faith, there may be an instantaneous cleansing and eradication of all sin from the heart of the believer by the baptism with the Holy Ghost and fire.

So the controversy resolves itself into the question at the head of this article. Some have supposed that this inbred sin was removed in regeneration, but this is contrary to the experience of all Christians in all ages, and is contrary to the teachings of the Bible. While the Apostle Paul could say of the Corinthians, "I thank my God always on your behalf, for the grace of God which is given you by Jesus Christ," and called them "babes in Christ," he also declared, "ye are yet carnal." (Cor. 3:3), which proves most conclusively that the carnal mind was not eradicated at the time of their conversion.

Others seem to think that by some mysterious process of growth the soul may advance until in some inexplicable manner, just about the time death might ensue, it would develop into a state of perfect holiness, and so have deliverance from the evil within. Just how, or by what law, the growth of a child would remove uncleanness, or the growth of the vegetable in the garden would at the same time grow out or destroy the weeds in the garden, is not explained. However, in the advancement of this theory there is the recognition of the sin-nature remaining in the heart after regeneration. Though the deliverance from it were only fully realized and accomplished at the time of death, it would nevertheless be a second or subsequent experience to regeneration.

Paul seemed to anticipate the repression theory in Rom. 6:1, 2, when he exclaimed: "What shall we say then? Shall we continue in sin, that grace may abound? God forbid. How shall we, that are dead to sin, live any longer therein?" He then continues by declaring that the divine method for inbred sin—"our old man," or, "the body of sin"—is crucifixion and destruction. "Knowing this, that our old man is crucified with him, that the body of sin might be destroyed." "Crucified" and "destroyed" surely does not mean repressed.

There is nothing that can eradicate sin from the heart but the blood of Jesus. If the blood is efficacious to cleanse from inbred sin when the person is dying, surely it has the same efficacy prior to death. Thank God for the promise, "If we walk in the light, as He is in the light, we have fellowship one with another, and the blood of Jesus Christ, His Son, cleanseth *us from all sin.*"

SANCTIFICATION AND THE BAPTISM WITH THE HOLY GHOST.

Whoever is sanctified wholly has the baptism with the Holy Ghost; whoever has the baptism with the Holy Ghost is sanctified wholly. It is the baptism with the Holy Ghost that sanctifies wholly. These terms simply represent different phases of the same experience, and are used as synonyms. When the consecration of the believer is entire and complete, the "old man," or inbred sin is crucified and eradicated by the baptism with the Holy Ghost. The negative side of sanctification, which is the destruction and removal of inbred sin, is as certainly effected by the Holy Ghost as is the positive side of sanctification, which is the divine infilling and the enduement of power. Multitudes are praying for power and so insist on having the positive side of sanctification without consenting to have the negative work of cleansing accomplished in them. All such seeking is in vain. The work of subtracting inbred sin from the heart must precede addition or the enduement of power. Purity is power.

In Acts, 15:8-9, we find that God gave to the house of Cornelius, under the preaching of Peter, exactly the same experience He had given the Apostles on the day of Pentecost. Or, in other words, exactly the same thing took place on the day of Pentecost that took place at the house of Cornelius. Peter says, God gave them the Holy Ghost, "And put no difference between us and them purifying their hearts by faith." So we see clearly that the Pentecostal blessing—the baptism with the Holy Ghost—does not simply mean the empowering for service but the *purifying of the heart by faith*. And we also see that in connection with the purifying of the heart—which is obtained by faith—the Holy Ghost is given. Sanctification comprehends both the *act* of purifying the heart and what may be termed the *result* of being thus purified, namely, that of being filled with the Holy Ghost. The Holy Ghost is sure to take up his abode in a clean heart.

We have known a preacher to preach on the baptism with the Holy Ghost, and emphasize the "power for service" feature, and many who had been professing the experience of sanctification presented themselves at the altar; either such persons had never been wholly sanctified, or else they were greatly confused and misled. As well go to the altar for the quickening and impartation of life, after having obtained pardon and being born again, as go to the altar seeking for the baptism with the Holy Ghost after having been purified and sanctified. As the pardon and quickening of the sinner take place simultaneously, so in like manner the purifying and sanctifying of the heart of the believer and the baptism with the Holy Ghost take place simultaneously. To have a pure heart is to have the Holy Ghost; to have the baptism with the Holy Ghost in the Pentecostal sense is to have the heart purified by faith. The receiving of the Holy Ghost and the purifying of the heart were not separate on the day of Pentecost, and must never be separated. It is possible that the *manifestation of the Holy* Spirit's fullness and presence may not come to the consciousness of the individual at the same instant in which faith claims the purifying of the heart—for the Holy Spirit can come into the heart without exciting the emotions—but we insist that the purifying and sanctifying of the heart and the baptism with the Holy Ghost occur simultaneously. It will be remembered that this experience is always subsequent to regeneration, since Jesus emphasized and qualified in John, 14:17, saying of the gift of the Holy Ghost, "Whom the world cannot receive." A man is of the "world" until after he is born again. "Have ye received the Holy Ghost since ye believed?" was exactly the equivalent of asking, "Have ye been sanctified wholly since you were converted?"

ENTIRE SANCTIFICATION NECESSARY TO ENTIRE SATISFACTION.

Man's normal condition, as God made him, is that of holiness. "God created man in His own image, in the image of God created He him." Sin produces an abnormal condition. Sin in the heart is a foreign substance—something that does not belong there. What a grain of sand would be to the eye, sin is to the heart. Hence it afflicts, and brings unrest and discontent. This is one reason why a sinner can never know rest and contentment. He scarcely realizes or recognizes the source of his trouble, but he knows there is always something he thinks he wants, which he does not now have. He fondly imagines if he could but have more pleasure, or more prominence, or more wealth, he would be satisfied, and so he presses on in pursuit of these things, only to find that those things simply mock the sad cry of his soul, increase the restlessness and discontent, and ever leave an aching void within. Like the man addicted to the use of strong drink, the more he drinks, the more he wants, and the more intense the craving becomes. God says, "Wherefore do ye spend money for that which is not bread; and your labor *for that which satisfieth not?*" "The wicked are like the troubled sea, when it cannot rest, whose waters cast up mire and dirt. There is no peace, saith my God to the wicked."

Until a man regains holiness, there is ever a conscious want or lack. God never intended a man should be satisfied without holiness, and consequently he never can be. Sanctification being the act of grace whereby we are made holy, it is not difficult to see that entire sanctification is necessary to entire satisfaction. As the Psalmist expressed it, "I shall be satisfied when I awake with Thy likeness." Holiness is the divine likeness. "He satisfieth the longing soul, and filleth the hungry soul with goodness." An experience that does not fully satisfy us never fully satisfies God.

At times we hear people say, after seeking for a time, "Perhaps I am expecting too much." Such a one needs to be reminded that the divine resources are unlimited, and inexhaustible, and that God has pledged His word, to fill and satisfy the longing, hungry soul. "They shall be *abundantly* satisfied." (Psa. 36:8.)

The difference of the craving and longing of a justified soul and that of a sanctified soul may be illustrated by the person having a craving or appetite for apple dumplings, or some special dish,—he may sit up to a table laden with good things, and eat all he may wish; but that one dish he was especially craving is not on the table; although he has had a full meal, he is still craving something not contained in that meal. Thus it is with the justified soul; he may be blessed even to the shouting point, and still crave something not contained in that blessing. But when he is sanctified wholly he gets the apple dumplings, or the very thing he was craving. That special longing having been satisfied, having received not only all he wanted, but the very thing his nature craved—his hungering and thirsting is just as though he had apple dumplings for every meal. Thus it is with the sanctified soul. He is not wanting or desiring something other than what he has, although at the next meal time he will relish some more of the same kind. Because justification does not and cannot satisfy the longing of the heart for holiness, they try so-called "innocent" and "no-harm" amusements, etc., and back-slide. Whereas, if they were properly instructed, and would seek entire sanctification, they would find what their heart is craving, and hence have entire satisfaction.

ENTIRE SANCTIFICATION—HOW OBTAINED

Three points, clearly and fully determined, will invariably bring the diligent seeker into the experience of entire sanctification.

First, there should be the positive assurance, or witness of the spirit to a present acceptance with God. If there is any doubt concerning this point—any questioning as to the pardon of all past sins, this point should be fully settled first. Many have found difficulty in seeking this experience because they were living beneath the plane where sanctification begins. We have observed that they who live in the clear light of justification are ever the first to seek this experience and seldom have any difficulty in receiving the same. Persons who are backsliders in heart, and are conscious that they are "sinning every day," are not eligible to this experience. If there is any sense of guilt and condemnation the prayer must be for pardon and reclamation and not for sanctification. But when the question of pardon and acceptance is fully settled, then it is time to drive a stake and say, "Glory," and take the second step toward sanctification.

Second. The second step toward entire sanctification is entire consecration—a complete and unconditional abandonment of yourself and your all to God. In Matt. 23:19, we read that it is "the altar that sanctifieth the gift." Christ being our living altar we need to dedicate and consecrate our all,—unconditionally, irrevocably and eternally—to him. This is the most difficult part in seeking the experience of sanctification. Usually there are three stages or three steps before consecration is completed. 1. "I desire to consecrate." 2. "I am trying to consecrate." 3. "I do give up all to Jesus." Some itemize their consecration; this is a good thing to do. However, there should be a large space between the itemized account and the signature of the individual with the understanding that God can fill out the blank space as it may seem good in His sight. Another plan is simply to emphasize the words "my all"—all I know and all I don't know; all I have and all I expect to have; all I am and all I hope to be; my past, present and future I yield to thee." The soul that desires the blessing more than anything else in the world and will make a death-bed consecration is very near the blessing. Consecration is the pledge of an eternal "yes" to all the will of God. Satan will be present to suggest that possibly all is not yet consecrated, but a resolute steadfast purpose of heart to be wholly the Lord's will speedily defeat the enemy. The singing of the following verse of consecration has helped multitudes into the experience:

"Here I give my all to Thee,
  Friends and time and earthly store;
Soul and body thine to be,
  Wholly thine forevermore."

When the soul can look up into heaven and say, "O my God thou knowest all things, ' and thou knowest my heart and my thoughts: thou dost know that I give up my all to thee; all I know and all that I do not know, which may be made known to me in the future," the blessing of sanctification is nigh at hand, there being but one more short step to be taken.

Third, When the foregoing steps have been taken—so that there is no lingering doubt regarding those points, it only remains for the seeker to exercise a little faith—appropriating faith—which appropriates the promises and receives the blessing God has promised. Faith is simply believing what God says, and believing it because God said it, and so making the promise our own. We may encourage our faith by determining the following three points: 1. God is *able* to sanctify me wholly. 2. God is *willing* to sanctify me wholly. 3. God is *ready* to sanctify me wholly. If God is now able, willing and ready to sanctify me wholly, and I am willing and ready to be sanctified wholly, what is to hinder? I *can,* and I *will* and I *do* now believe that Jesus sanctifies me wholly. I have done my part, I now believe He does His part. My case is wholly in His hands: I now trust Jesus to sanctify me wholly. I do now receive Jesus as my sanctifier, and trust His blood to cleanse my heart from all sin."

> "Hallelujah 'tis done,
> I believe on the Son,
> I am saved by the blood
> Of the crucified One."

Now there is nothing more to do but rest on the promises, and believe that the blood of Jesus now cleanseth *me* from all sin, because Jesus says so, and praise Him for the cleansing. If the enemy continues to buffet, declare your faith to others; tell them that you believe that the blood of Jesus cleanseth your heart from all sin; that you have, and do now receive Jesus as your sanctifier, and the victory is complete. "They overcame him (Satan) by the blood of the Lamb, and by the word of their testimony; and they loved not their lives unto the death." Rev. 12:11. "Sanctified by faith." Acts 26:18.

SOME BENEFITS OF SANCTIFICATION.

THE BENEFITS of sanctification are innumerable, and we can only hope to mention a few of them.

First. *Clarified Vision*: "After that He put His hands again upon His eyes, and made him look up: and he was restored and saw every man clearly." After this man had received one touch he could see, but not clearly; he said, "I see men as trees walking." A second touch was positively necessary in his case, in order that he might see "clearly." We have heard of a man who had obtained the blessing of sanctification by a second experience, saying he had found a new version of the Scripture. So it has seemed to many; before being sanctified they had failed to see much in the Bible relating to sanctification or the second blessing, but after having received the experience they could see it taught in almost every chapter, and almost everywhere in the Bible. The Bible had not changed, but after having received the second touch they were enabled to "see clearly."

Jesus taught in the sermon on the mount that purity of heart—which is the result of entire sanctification—would effect the vision. "Blessed are the pure in heart; for they shall see—God." Not only see God in heaven, but see Him now, in His word, in His people, in nature, in His providences—everywhere they can see God. In all the things that were formerly attributed to luck, or a happen-so, or a mysterious providence, the pure in heart will now see God, in His love, or justice, or faithfulness, or mercy, etc. They can now see God in everything and everything in God. "Anoint thine eyes with eyesalve, that thou mayest see."

Second. *Stability*: "By whom also we have access by faith into this grace *wherein we stand.*" The cause of the fluctuating, evanescent, up and down experience of multitudes, is inbred sin in the heart. The Lord removes the cause of this "wobbling" by sanctifying us wholly. Wherever the preserving grace is mentioned, as in 1 Thess. 5: 24 and Jude 1:1, it is invariably preceded by and coupled with the sanctifying grace. "Sanctified by God the Father, and preserved." As a good house-wife would not undertake to preserve fruit without first removing every speck and decayed spot, so in like manner Jesus would first sanctify and cleanse us from all sin, and then preserve us -blameless. Preserved means done up so you keep. And God's preserves will keep in all climates, in all seasons of the year and under all circumstances. "The very God of peace sanctify you wholly; and I pray

God your whole spirit and soul and body be preserved blameless unto the coming of our Lord Jesus Christ Faithful is He that calleth you *who also will do it."*

Third. *Preparation for service*: "A vessel unto honor, sanctified, and meet for the Master's use, and prepared unto every good work." 2 Tim. 2:21. According to this passage sanctification is the preparation for every good work. The Apostles were not fully qualified for their life's work until after they received the purification of their hearts by the baptism with the Holy Ghost on the day of Pentecost, as a second distinct experience. "Every branch that beareth fruit, He purgeth it, that it may bring forth more fruit." Here it would seem that the great object of the purging is "more fruit." The moment the prophet Isaiah had been touched by the live coal from off the altar and heard it said "thine iniquity is taken away, and thy sin purged," the language of his heart was, "here am I; send me." He did not keep his seat, because he wanted to hear others speak, according to the phraseology common in many class meetings; nor did he ask the Lord to send some one else, because they had more talent and better ability to talk, but he at once was ready to do whatever God might permit him to do. "And purify unto Himself a peculiar people, *zealous of good works."* Purity precedes the zeal for good works. Sanctified people are not only prepared, but anxious to do anything the Lord would have them do. Having deliverance and rest from inward struggle with inberd sin, and its various manifestations,—no more a wrestling with "flesh and blood,"—the sanctified soul now has a heart and hand free to help others. Before being sanctified wholly it required all the energy and time to keep ourselves straight, with but little disposition or grace to help others.

SANCTIFICATION THE CURE FOR UNBELIEF.

Perfect love brings perfect confidence. This is true in everything. Perfect love means complete devotement, and complete devotement means cheerful obedience, and where there is the witness of the Spirit and the testimony of the conscience to perfect obedience there is boldness and assurance. "If our heart condemn us not, then have we confidence toward God."

The child who has disobeyed the parent cannot ask a favor of the parent in confidence, because of the accusations of its conscience. The man who has violated the law seeks to evade the officer of the law because he feels self-condemned. So when the heart is not fully assured that God is pleased it cannot approach Him in perfect confidence.

Unbelief has its root and source in carnality; the carnal mind not being "subject to the law of God," destroys confidence and so generates doubt and unbelief; hence every unsanctified soul has more or less of conflict with unbelief. Many have supposed unbelief simply a weakness, but not so; it is a devilishness; it dishonors God and imperils the soul. Faith honors God and "is the victory that overcometh the world."

Uubelief is the tap-root of all evil; faith is the avenue of every blessing. Sanctification is faith made easy, as by this experience the soul is brought into an atmosphere and condition where the hindrances to faith are all removed. Believe God and you will find a pure heart; having a pure heart you will find it most natural and easy to believe God, and live the life of faith.

GROWING INTO SANCTIFICATION.

Growing into sanctification is as unreasonable as it is unscriptural. While there is a growth *in* grace, there is no such a thing as growing *into* grace. As well speak of a child having a soiled face growing clean, or of growing weeds out of a garden as talk of growing impurity and carnality out of the heart. Sanctification is a "divine act"—a work that is divinely inwrought by the Holy Ghost, and therefore can never be *attained,* but must be *obtained* by faith. "Wherefore Jesus also, that He might sanctify the people with His own blood, suffered without the gate." It is a work that Jesus proposes to do for you and in you. To this there are thousands who will bear glad testimony; but never have we known of one person who could or would bear testimony that he had reached sanctification by growth. If it were by growth, there would of necessity be degrees of sanctification, and to be true to the facts some would need to testify that they were *little* sanctified; others that they were *more* sanctified; and still others that they were *most* sanctified. How absurd! However, after the "divine act" of sanctification in which inbred sin is eradicated, the "old man" crucified, there is unstinted and limitless growth. When anger, and fear, and pride, and all the roots of bitterness are removed there is just the condition of growth, just as when the weeds are removed from a garden the vegetables will grow. There will be more real development and advance in one week after being wholly sanctified than there is previous to sanctification in a month. Sanctification is essential to real growth.

SANCTIFICATION AND MISTAKES.

Sanctification is not infallibility. A pure heart does not mean a perfect head. Sanctified people make mistakes. A mistake is a thing of the head; a sin is a thing of the heart. A mistake is the thing you do because you do not know better; sin is the thing you do when you do know better. In confounding the two, many persons have become confused, and have cast away their confidence.

The Standard Dictionary defines a mistake as "an error in action, judgment or preception. * * * An unintentional wrong act or step." Men may be perfectly honest and sincere and yet err in judgment. Having wrong premises they will arrive at wrong conclusions, even though the heart is pure and the motive right. We have known of a case where a mother gave to her child a glass containing a medicine which was rank poison, thinking the glass contained nothing but pure water. This was a very sad and grievous mistake, almost costing the life of the child; and the mother, becoming nearly distracted and frenzied with grief, was but an object of pity and sympathy. It was simply and purely a mistake—"an unintentional wrong act." This was not an evidence that the mother did not have a pure heart. Had she given that child that glass with knowledge and intent, it would have been a heinous sin, and would have merited and received the just condemnation and wrath of God. It would have been murder in the first degree, so far as the mother was concerned even though the child survived, and the community believed it to be a mistake. Motive determines the morality of the act. Not always knowing the motives of men, it is best not to take the judgment seat, lest we adjudge that as sin which was wholly a mistake, or, that as a mistake which God knows to be sin. "Man looketh on the outward appearance, but the Lord looketh on the heart." "The Lord searcheth all hearts, and understandeth all the imaginations of the thoughts."

We can see by the foregoing how that which might be a mistake on the part of one would be a sin on the part of others, and vice versa. Of course, where a mistake occurs because of negligence on the part of those committing the mistake, such mistake is not wholly inexcusable. However, in such case the act is not to be so much condemned as the negligence or failure to properly inform one's self when said information was at hand.

While sanctified people are liable to mistakes because of mental infirmities and ignorance it is nevertheless true that the liabilities are not so great, and the mistakes perhaps not so numerous, owing to the fact that they are walking in the clear light of God, and hence have keener discernment, a clearer vision, and quicker moral preceptions. A man walking in the clear light of the noonday sun is certainly not as liable to stumble as he who walks in the shadows. Herein is one advantage in being wholly sanctified.

Doubtless because some men have failed to distinguish between mistakes and sin, they have concluded they could not live the sanctified life, and so, naturally concluded no one else could. And because of this failure to note this distinction the holy people and the holiness movement in general have been greatly discounted and misjudged, and so condemned by men, where God approved. Our mistakes should be a source of humiliation to us, and make us to feel our own unworthiness, and the need of the atoning blood. No, sanctified people do not claim to be infallible.

SANCTIFICATION AND HOLY LIVING.

A holy heart is the condition for and secret of living a holy life. To undertake to live a holy life with an unholy heart is to undertake the impossible. An impure fountain can only send forth an impure stream. To deny the privilege and possibility of having a pure heart and yet demand a holy life is unreasonable, unscriptural and tyrannical. No man is better than his heart, no matter what his profession or pretenses may be. "Doth a fountain send forth at the same place sweet water and bitter? Can the fig tree, my brethren, bear olive berries? Either a vine, figs? So can no fountain both yield salt water and fresh."

Human religions begin on the outside and take for their slogan, "Do right and you will be right." In this the Pharisees were adepts, so much so that Jesus said of them, "Ye make clean the outside of the cup and platter, but within they are full of extortion and excess." According to this a man may have a clean outward life and yet be none other than a Pharisee. "Except your righteousness shall exceed the righteousness of the scribes and Pharisees, ye shall in no case enter into the Kingdom of Heaven." The religion of Jesus Christ begins with the heart, and says: "Thou blind Pharisee, cleanse first that which is within the cup and platter that the outside of them may be clean also." A good man out of the good treasure of his heart bringeth forth that which is good."

The enemy keeps many people out of the blessing of sanctification by telling them that because of their peculiar temperament and their environments, they could never live a holy life. This is all a delusion and device of Satan to deceive and defeat a hungry soul. Sanctification will correct your peculiar temperament and lift you above conditions and environments and enable you to "reign in life." There can be nothing more easy or more natural than for a man to live out what is in him. Be right and you will do right. Sanctification is religion made easy and brings a life of glad victory.

Many seem to think that God has laid down two standards of living—one for the justified and another for the sanctified, and so may be heard to excuse themselves for some unholy indulgence of temper or appetite, by saying they never professed sanctification, as though the refusal to walk in the light and be cleansed from all sin gave one license to live beneath the standard of holiness. This, too, is a delusion. God requires holiness of all men regardless of what they profess or do not profess. God does not wait for a man to subscribe his name to the ten commandments before he requires obedience to the same. A sanctified man has a right to do anything anyone else has a right to do. No man has right or liberty to do anything that is wrong. A justified man should walk just as straight and live just as consistent and obedient before God as a sanctified man. God says to all men: "Be ye holy, for I am holy."

The beauty of sanctification is that it removes from the heart everything that is antagonistic to a holy life, and puts His Spirit within you, which will "cause" you to walk in his statutes and keep His judgments and do them."—Ezek. 36:27.

Another thrust of the enemy is to say to those professing the blessing of sanctification: "You need not say anything about it, *just live it.*" This is like saying to a white man, "Now be a white man." If you have the blessing, of course you will live it. If you do not live it, you cannot long testify to the blessing, and if you do not testify to the blessing, you will soon cease to live it, for you will not long possess the blessing when you cease to testify to the same. Life and testimony must go together. God says, "Ye are my witnesses." "They overcame him by the blood of the Lamb, and by the word of their testimony."

SANCTIFICATION AND STABILITY.

While the Bible teaches the possibility of losing the grace of God out of the heart—hence the necessity of constant watchfulness—it also teaches that it is gloriously possible for a man to have the grace of God and ever retain it. While a man may lose it, he also may keep it. There is no necessity of falling if there is a compliance with the conditions for standing. But the plain teaching of the Bible is, that the *"whole armour"* is necessary as a safeguard against the foe; that he who has neglected or failed to "put on the whole armour of God" has not availed himself of the necessary equipment to stand, and therefore has no assurance of standing; and "if after they have escaped the pollutions of the world through the knowledge of the Lord and Savior Jesus Christ, they are again entangled therein, and overcome, the latter end is worse with them than the beginning."

By "the whole armour of God" is doubtless meant full salvation, or the full provisions of the Gospel.

It is a fact that is noteworthy that the sanctifying grace invariably precedes preserving grace, as in Jude 1:1 —"Sanctified by God the Father, *and preserved* in Jesus Christ." Also in 1 Thess. 5:23-24, "The very God of peace sanctify you wholly: and I pray God your whole spirit and soul and body be preserved blameless." First sanctified wholly and then preserved blameless. As the good house-wife preserves only fruit that is sound and whole—first cutting out all the specks and spots and core—so in like manner the Lord puts up His preserves, by the baptism with the Holy Ghost and fire, consuming all dross and every "root of evil," and so making us every whit whole. God does not propose to preserve men with sin in their hearts; He first cleanses the heart from all sin by the baptism with the Holy Ghost and fire, and then preserves blameless.

In Rom. 5:2 we read of it as the *standing grace,* or, "This grace wherein we stand," because it enables one not only to endure hardness, and patiently suffer, and "rejoice in hope of the glory of God," but actually enables those who have it to "glory in tribulations also." As indicated by the word *"also,"* it is a grace obtained subsequent to "being justified by faith." The mistake made by a great many is to suppose that this grace can only be realized as the result of a long drawn out process of growth —as a gradual attainment. But the text says, "By whom also we have access *by faith,* into this grace wherein we stand." Seeing it may be obtained by faith, there can be no reason why it should not be a present tense experience with every Christian.

Until "this grace wherein we stand" is earnestly sought and obtained, the believer has not reached the place where he can say, "having done all to stand;" to reject, or neglect to "put on the whole armour of God," the sanctifying grace, "this grace wherein we stand," is to greatly imperil the soul, and be continually living an up and down, unstable and unsatisfactory life. As the foundations of a house preserve the house, so, in turn, the house preserves the foundation; so the sanctifying grace preserves our justification. "We are made partakers of Christ, if we hold the beginning of our confidence steadfast unto the end." (Heb. 3:14.)

SANCTIFICATION AND POWER.

There are many persons who are ready to seek for a "baptism of power," or "power for service," who are averse and antagonistic to sanctification, and stoutly deny the teaching of a second experience. We insist that the secret of Pentecostal power is a Pentecostal experience; and the Pentecostal experience is an experience given to believers, and not to sinners, and, therefore, necessarily is a second experience, marking a second crisis, or epoch in the life of such as receive it.

This was so with the disciples in connection with the historic Pentecost, as recorded in the second chapter of the Acts. They had been "born of God" and had received "power to become the sons of God," (John 1:12, 13), and had heard Jesus say unto them, "Behold I give unto you power to tread on serpents and scorpions, and *over all the power of the enemy,* (Luke 10:19) and had walked with Jesus three years in closest fellowship, themselves healing the sick, casting out devils, and had the testimony of Jesus, saying, "They are not of the world, even as I am not of the world;" "they have kept thy word;" "those that thou gavest me I have kept, and none of them is lost," excepting Judas; "they are thine. And all mine are thine, and thine are mine; and I am glorified in them;" and when He ascended to the Father, He "blessed them," "and they worshipped him, and returned to Jerusalem with great joy and were continually in the temple, praising and blessing God:" and yet they had the commandment of Jesus, spoken just before He ascended, saying, "But tarry ye in the city of Jerusalem, until ye be endued with power from on high."—Luke 24:49. This promise had its literal fulfillment on the day of Pentecost.

Nowhere in the Bible do we read of a "baptism of power," or of "power for service," but we do read, "This is the will of God, even your sanctification." Sanctification negatively stated is the entire devotement and setting apart of our all to God, and the eradication and destruction of inbred sin—the sin-nature which we inherited—thus purifying the heart; but the positive side of sanctification is the in-filling with the Holy Ghost, accompanied by the enduement of power. It is impossible for a man to be filled with the Holy Ghost without having the power of the Holy Ghost, and it is impossible to be filled with the Holy Ghost, in the Pentecostal sense, without being cleansed and purified from inbred sin; and it is impossible to be thus cleansed and purified from inbred sin and filled with the Holy Ghost until after the soul has been pardoned and regenerated. For in giving the promise of the Holy Ghost, Jesus said of Him, "Whom the world cannot receive."—John 14:17. A man is of the world until he is born again and adopted into God's family; then and not until then is he eligible to the gift of the Holy Ghost.

To state the case more plainly: The secret of power is the indwelling Holy Ghost in his Pentecostal fullness; the Holy Ghost himself is the power; this gift of the Holy Ghost cannot be received by "the world" or a sinner, and therefore must be a second experience; and this infilling with the Holy Ghost and enduement with power, which is clearly the *positive* side of sanctification, cannot be received without the *negative* work of entire devotement of our all to God, and entire purification from inbred sin.

Hence to get sanctified wholly is to get the pre-pentecost promise. The negative and the positive side of sanctification occur simultaneously.

Seeking power for service is almost the equivalent to asking for the Holy Ghost, in order that we might use Him; instead, we should be so utterly and completely abandoned to Him that He might use us. Amen.

SANCTIFICATION AND REVIVALS.

God's method for saving the world is by and through the sanctification of His people. Jesus prayed "Sanctify them," "that they all may be one," *"that the world may believe."* (John 17:17-21.) According to this prayer, sanctification is essential to that unity of His people, which is imperative, and the condition for saving the world. Hence, he who opposes or is indifferent to the subject of sanctification virtually is in opposition to the divine method for saving the world. This will explain why preachers antagonistic to sanctification as a distinct experience, do not see many sinners converted.

By seventeen years of continuous experience as an evangelist, laboring in many states, and among more than a score of denominations, thus having tested this matter under all conditions and circumstances, I have demonstrated that wherever believers are sanctified wholly, sinners will be converted. Never have I known this to fail. The sure way and short cut to precipitating a revival is to have believers sanctified.

Mr. Wesley wrote: "Indeed, this I always observe,—wherever a work of sanctification breaks out, the whole work of God prospers. Some are convinced of sin, others justified, and all stirred up to greater earnestness for salvation."—*Journal*, Aug., 1775. Again, in writing to Rev. John Baxendale, in 1875, he said: "Indeed, His work will flourish in every place where full sanctification is clearly and strongly preached."—*Works*, Vol. 6, p. 172, and again in Vol. 6, p. 721, Mr. Wesley said: "Where Christian perfection is not strongly and explicitly preached, there is seldom any remarkable blessing from God; and consequently little addition to the society, and little life in the members of it. . . . *Till you press the believers to expect full salvation now, you must not look for any revival.*"

The sanctification of one hundred and twenty *believers* by the baptism with the Holy Ghost on the day of Pentecost, instantly precipitated a revival such as the world had never witnessed, and resulted in the conversion of "about three thousand souls" the first day. Speaking to the disciples concerning this "second blessing,"—the gift of the Holy Ghost, Jesus said, "If I go not away, the Comforter will not come unto *you*; but if I depart, I will send him unto *you*. And when He is come (*unto you,* who are already converted) He will reprove the world of sin, and of righteousness and of judgment." John 16:7, 8. The sure and quick way to bring conviction and salvation to the unsaved, is for the church herself to seek and obtain the blessing of entire sanctification and so be filled with the Holy Ghost.

Men are constantly praying for the Holy Ghost that

they might use Him, but what is needed, is that believers so utterly devote and abandon themselves to Him, that He may purify and cleanse them from all sin, and then infill and use them. The sanctification of one believer often means the salvation of many souls.

To any pastor desiring a revival, we would like to offer the following receipt, and will unhesitatingly guarantee that where this receipt is followed out, a revival will take place: *To the pastor,*—If clearly justified, seek definitely until *you* obtain the distinct experience of entire sanctification; then bear public testimony to the same, without equivocation, and then preach definitely on' the subject of entire sanctification until at least six members of the congregation seek and obtain a definite experience of sanctification, and the revival, resulting in the conversion of sinners is assured. It has been tried many times and never known to fail.. "And the heathen shall know that I am the Lord, saith the Lord God, when I shall be sanctified in you before their eyes." Ezek. 36:23.

WITNESSING TO SANCTIFICATION.

FAITH is driving the nail, while testimony is the clinching of the nail, so far as the individual is concerned. One of the most effectual weapons for defeating the enemy is the public confession and declaration of faith. "They overcame him by the blood of the Lamb, *and by the word of their testimony."* Indeed, the faith that saves and the declaration of the same are inseparably connected in the

Scripture. "For with the heart man believeth unto righteousness; and with the mouth confession is made unto salvation."

One of the most subtle devices of Satan is to suggest to the soul who has recently entered the blessing of sanctification that "it is not necessary that much be said about it; simply live it." "If you will but live it, people will know that you are sanctified, and there will be no occasion to tell them so." Especially are these expressions common where there is antagonism to the doctrine, the enemy knowing full well that where the testimony is withheld the experience cannot be long retained.

The facts are, life and lip must go together. He who will not confess the God-given experience will soon have no experience to confess. He who will not confess it will not long live it; and he who will not live it, cannot long confess it. The life and the testimony go hand in hand. The sad experience and testimony of multitudes has been that they have lost the experience because they failed to definitely witness to the same. The Lord says: "And it shall be, when thou art come in unto the land (Canaan) which the Lord thy God giveth thee for an inheritance, and possessest it, and dwellest therein; that thou shalt take of the first of all the fruit of the earth which thou shalt bring of thy land that the Lord thy God giveth thee, and shalt put it in a basket, and shalt go unto the place where the Lord thy God shall choose to place His name there. And thou shalt go unto the priest that shall be in those days, and say unto him, *I profess this day unto the Lord thy God, that I am come unto the country* which the Lord sware unto our fathers for to give us."—Deut. 26:1-3. Here we see the divine order is to fill the basket with the fruit, and then *"profess."* It was not enough to simply show the fruit; they must also *"profess."*

The reasons for giving public testimony are manifold. First, if God has wrought the work we should publicly acknowledge it in order to give Him all the glory. That men may know it is He, and not we ourselves who had effected the change. Men would ascribe the glory to us, or to conditions, or change of circumstances, hence we need continually "declare His doings among the people," and "make mention that His name is exalted." Second, public testimony is the perfecting and clinching of the faith of the individual, and so gives the victory over the adversary. Third, it is the divine method for acquainting others with their privileges. This is one of the objects of the blessing: "Ye shall receive power, after that the Holy Ghost is come upon you: *and ye shall be witnesses unto me."* A witness is supposed to *tell* what he knows; and the more controverted the matter is, the more important it is that there should be reliable witnesses, to tell what they know, in order to confirm the truth. "That in the mouth of two or three witnesses every word may be established."

It is not proper to say "I am holy," or, "I am sanctified," etc., but we should always place Jesus foremost in the testimony; certainly no one could reasonably object to a man saying, "Jesus has cleansed my heart from all sin," or, "Jesus has sanctifed me wholly," etc.

There is great blessing and reward in public confession. Jesus has said, "Whosoever therefore shall confess me before men, him will I confess also before My Father which is in heaven." On condition that we stand for Him and represent Him on earth, He agrees to stand for us and represent us in heaven.

SANCTIFICATION, OR "CALL IT WHAT YOU PLEASE."

There are those who tell us "there is nothing in a name," and that they "are not sticklers for terms," etc., all of which is misleading and a subterfuge of Satan. If there is nothing in a name what occasion is there to have any name for anything or anybody? If there is "nothing in a name," why does not some one name a new-born child Jezebel or Judas Iscariot? Even a so-called infidel or atheist would not consent to have a child thus named. After all, there is something in a name.

We know that in the Old Testament, names were used which were significant and indicative of character; and if in this our day the names given do not indicate the character of the child who must wear the name, it is very often indicative of the character of those who gave the name, to-wit: Religious people most frequently give to their children some Bible name, or the name of some one who has been prominent in the religious world. For instance, it is safe to suppose that the parents of a child, who had as a part of its cognomen the name Wesley, were inclined toward Methodism, if not themselves in the enjoyment of Methodist religion. It would indicate that they were admirers of Wesley, and therefore must be Arminian in faith, etc.

It is only in the advocacy of the experience and doctrine of entire sanctification that men wax so liberal as to say, "Call it what you please;" or "I don't care what you call it." This, so-called, broad and liberal method of speaking of the experience of sanctification would not be permissible or tolerated in other matters. Very few parents would be ready to say to the community at large, concerning their own children, "Call them what you please," or "I don't care what you call them." No, they would insist that the name they themselves had given the children should be recognized. And so it should be.

Then what right have we to speak of an experience which God Himself has named, by some other name than that given by Himself? The fact that the name may not be a popular one, or does not meet with our fancy, would surely not justify us in trying to change the name, or in saying, "Call it what you please." While we may not insist on the use of just one term, we would insist that it is most consistent and proper to use the terms found in the Bible, and so call the experience God has given by the names He has given to the experience. To speak of the experience of sanctification as a "deeper work of grace," or a "higher life," or "a great blessing," etc., may be beautifully indefinite, and not occasion offense to anyone, save the Spirit, but it is always evasive, and an evidence that there is yet an unwillingness to go without the camp and bear His reproach. Jesus said, "Whosoever shall be ashamed of Me *and of My words,* of him shall the Son of Man be ashamed."

We have heard it said, by those who declare there is nothing in a name, that "a rose would be just as beautiful and fragrant if called by some other name." While that may be true, we would nevertheless insist that it would be very misleading—and an evidence of ignorance or willful deception—to call a rose a dandelion or a pumpkin vine, or "Call it what you please." Unless you call it a rose, no one would be likely to know what was meant. While it might not effect the rose to call it by some other name, it would certainly affect anyone who might be desiring or seeking for a rose. So it is certain only they who use the definite terms of the Scripture succeed in leading persons into the experience indicated by those terms. Hence it is that when men preach sanctification in a vague, indefinite manner, no one knows what they are talking about—no one is offended—and no one seeks and obtains the experience.

Zachariah's mouth was never opened until he called his child by the name God himself had given. But when he wrote, "His name is John," "his mouth was opened immediately, and his tongue loosed, and he spake and praised God." Give the child the name that God has given—"sanctification," "holiness," "perfect love," etc., and people will know what you are talking about. Amen! There is perhaps no word in the English language the devil hates more tremendously and that God loves and blesses more abundantly than the uncompromising use of the word "Sanctification." When people do not love this term, it is invariably because they lack the experience. As soon as the experience is obtained the word ceases to be objectionable and becomes most delightful and attractive.

IF SANCTIFIED, HOW COULD A PERSON SIN?

This is a question which seems to distress some people very much. They ask the question with that seriousness that would give the impression that they would regard it a great calamity and misfortune should one become so thoroughly saved as to be entirely free from sin. The inference is that they desire a little license or liberty to sin occasionally, should they desire so to do, hence they would not be willing to have the Lord sanctify them, and thus deprive them of this privilege. Of such we can only say, there is no occasion for their being exercised on the subject of sanctification. Such persons have not reached the place where sanctification begins. A person who has not yet fully abandoned and renounced all sin is not justified and therefore is no proper candidate for sanctification.

Touching the question, "If sanctified, how can a person sin?" we would answer, just as Adam and Eve, who were holy and in the image of God could sin; and just as angels who were holy and in the very presence of God in a holy heaven could sin, just so they who have been sanctified may again yield to temptation and fall into sin. Sanctification does not exempt men from temptation; and neither does sanctification destroy the free agency of man, and so change him into a machine. A sanctified man still has the exercise of his own free will, and hence has the power of choice, and therefore can choose that which is forbidden.

Because Adam and Eve yielded to temptation and thereby made a wrong choice, is not in evidence that they had not been created holy and in the image of God. If the reader will explain how holy angels could sin, and how Adam and Eve could sin, they will have explained how a sanctified person might sin.

Sanctified people do not say that they have not the power to sin, or could not sin if they wanted to, as they are frequently charged. But they do say that they have reached a place where they do not want to sin, and where they have power not to sin, and where there is no occasion or necessity to commit sin. In the language of John Wesley to Miss Jane Hilton: "Two things are certain: the one, that it is possible to lose even the pure love of God; the other, that *it is not necessary,* it is not unavoidable; it may be lost, *but it may be kept."—Works, vol. 7, p.* 43.

However, sanctified people have just as much right to commit sin as people who are not sanctified. No one has license or liberty to commit sin. "He that committeth sin is of the devil." We do not teach that men should seek sanctification in order to quit sinning; a person has to turn from and forsake all sin before God will ever hear him and pardon him. "If I regard iniquity in my heart, the Lord will not hear me." A man must go out of the sin business before God will ever save him. Genuine conviction and repentance will result in the abhorrence and forsaking of all sin.

"What then is the advantage in being sanctified?" Much every way; while there is yet the possibility of a man losing this grace out of his heart and committing sin, the inward responses to the temptations of Satan without, have ceased in the sanctified soul, hence the probabilities and liabilities to commit sin are not near so great, as where there is evil within *and* a foe without. When inbred sin is eradicated, and the inward conflict has ended, there is a free hand to cope with the enemy without, and therefore victory more easy.

WHAT BECOMES OF PEOPLE WHO ARE NOT SANCTIFIED?

Sanctification is the act of divine grace whereby we are made holy. It is certain that nothing unholy can enter heaven. Hence we read, Heb. 12:14, "Follow after peace with all men, and the sanctification without which no man shall see the Lord." (Revised version). If Christ had not regarded our sanctification as necessary and essential to our salvation, He certainly would never have "suffered without the gate that he might sanctify the people with His own blood." (Heb. 13:12). The carnal mind or inbred sin is unholiness, and cannot enter heaven. Will God receive into heaven the carnal mind which is the very quintessence of enmity against Himself? Never. While justification gives us the right to heaven, it requires entire sanctification to give us the fitness for heaven. So the question, "May I not get to heaven without sanctification?" is not a proper question for any Christian to ask, seeing that without holiness no man shall see the Lord. The proper question Christians might ask is, How long can I refuse and reject holiness and still remain justified? No man is condemned or lost because he was born into this world with the carnal mind or inbred sin in him; but all men will be condemned and lost for rejecting the light and refusing to be sanctified wholly. "This is the condemnation, that light is come." The measure of our light is the measure of our responsibility. To refuse holiness is to disobey God; and disobedience is sin, and sin brings guilt and condemnation and death. A man is not condemned for having been born with sin in him; it is not the result of his volition, or an act of his part. This was transmitted to us by the laws of heredity as a result of Adam's disobedience; we are not condemned for something we have not done. Condemnation can only set in with reference to inbred sin, when we neglect and refuse to walk in the light, and so disobey God. Condemned, not for having inbred sin, but for disobedience in refusing deliverance from the same. Here is where many lose their justification and utterly backslide. A person under condemnation is not eligible to sanctification, but has need of pardon. Conviction of need and condemnation for disobedience are two different things.

But it is urged by some that their friends and loved ones had never heard it preached and so had not refused sanctification and yet they had certainly died triumphantly and gone to heaven. If they did not hear it preached and knew nothing about their privilege in this matter, then they did not disobey God by refusing and rejecting it; and here the case differs with that of the objector. We see that walking in the light is essential and the condition of continued justification. Whoever walks in all the light he has and so retains justification, unquestionably enters heaven. We will endeavor to illustrate this point by the explanation of another point. By way of illustration we will consider the infant in its innocency. All infants dying in innocency go to heaven, and yet it is true of all children, as David said of himself, "Behold, I was shapen in iniquity; and in sin did my mother conceive me." (Ps. 51:5). To condemn the babe for something it did not do, and knows nothing of, would be unjust; to receive it into heaven with the evil nature or carnal mind which was born in the child, would be to admit sin into heaven. So the only explanation or solution of the problem is, the child by virtue of its innocence, at the moment of its death, that had the unconditional benefit of the atonement and the application of the blood of Jesus to cleanse it from inbred sin, and then went sweeping through the gates. While we never had committed any sins, and so had no sins pardoned, it was cleansed by the blood of Jesus from inbred sin—the root of all sin—and so with all the redeemed. "Washed in the blood of the Lamb." Some urge that the babe is born pure, but in so saying, they rule the child out of the atonement; for if the child is born pure and dies in its innocency, it would need no Savior, nor atonement, nor shed blood, but would be pure by virtue of its birth.

So if a justified man has walked in all the light he has had, and has had no knowledge of his need or privilege of being cleansed from inbred sin, it would be unjust to condemn him for that which he did not do, and knows nothing of; on the other hand to take him into heaven with inbred sin would be to admit of sin into heaven; so we are compelled to concede and glad to believe that such have the unconditional cleansing from inbred sin at the moment of their death, by virtue of the fact that they had walked in all the light they had; not that death cleansed them, for death has no saving power, but at the moment of their death the blood of Jesus cleansed them from inbred sin, and they went sweeping through the gates washed in the blood of the Lamb. This has been designated as dying grace; but even in such a case, sanctification was a second experience. We may not wait to be cleansed at death because of the light that has come to us, the refusal of which would be disobedience and sin, and so would forfeit to us our justification. "If we walk in the light, as He is in the light, we have fellowship one with another, and the blood of Jesus Christ, His Son, cleanseth us from all sin." I. John, 1:7.

"I CANNOT SEE INTO SANCTIFICATION."

The caption of this article is an oft-repeated statement made by persons who hesitate in seeking the blessing of entire sanctification when urged to do so. By this they mean to say, they do not understand the subject, and therefore refuse to seek it.

To such we say, if a sinner refused to seek pardon until he could "see into it," and understand all about the *modus operandi*—he never would be saved. The facts are, no man can understand or explain all about the science or philosophy of the new birth, nor any other experience divinely inwrought. Nevertheless, multitudes who have believed and entered in, are glad witnesses to the glorious facts of a personal experience both to the regenerating and sanctifying power of God.

No man is required to "see into it," or understand all about it, either before or after the experience. One may understand little or nothing about surgery and yet may experience the amputation of a finger or some other member of the body. It is enough that he who performs the operation understands the how sufficiently to accomplish what needs to be done.

With most people it is not so much mental difficulties that keep them out of the experience, as it is heart difficulties; something the heart is not willing to yield to God. When persons are willing to "see into sanctification," it is not difficult to make them understand at least the theory of sanctification as a second experience.

To such an one we would simply point out the twofold nature of sin—sin as an act, committed, which requires repentance and pardon, and sin as a *nature* or principle inherited, innate, inborn, which requires *cleansing*. Sins committed may be forgiven, but the sin-nature inherited, cannot be forgiven, because it is not something we have done, or the result of any volition on our part; it was born in us, and it would be folly to ask God to forgive that out of us, or to ask God to forgive us for having been thus born. In the nature of things God cannot forgive me something I have not done, something which is not the result of my volition; while He cannot forgive inbred sin, He can nevertheless eradicate, destroy and cleanse out of the heart the very sin-nature, "and purify unto Himself a peculiar people, zealous of good works."

This is just what He proposes to do, and that brings an experimental knowledge of sanctification. Any one walking in the clear light of justification will soon discover within himself the presence of this "evil nature," manifesting itself in anger, pride, fear, doubt, unholy ambition, unholy appetites, &c., all of which is contrary to the new life, and thus become convinced of his need of this cleansing; this sense of need, with the knowledge that "This is the will of God, even your sanctification" is all that one needs to understand in order to obtain this glorious experience.

A person will know more in five minutes after receiving the experience than he could have known in ten years of reasoning and theorizing. "If any man will do His will he shall know of the doctrine." John 7:17.

DARKNESS AND HEAVINESS.

These terms are used by many professors as synonymous, but the Scriptures never use them interchangeably. While "heaviness" is compatible with holiness and fellowship with God, darkness is not. In 1 John 1:5, 6 we read, "God is light, and in Him is no darkness at all. If we say that we have fellowship with Him, and walk in darkness, we lie, and do not the truth." It is sin that brings darkness. Hence sin is spoken of as "the unfruitful works of darkness;" the soul redeemed by grace is said to have been called "out of darkness into His marvelous light."

Certain it is that sin beclouds the vision of the soul and shuts out the light of God. To say that a soul is in darkness is equivalent to saying that some sin has entered the heart and life, and so broken the fellowship between the soul and God, and consequently the soul is left to grope in darkness. Seeing that God cannot countenance sin, we can understand why God has said, "If we say that we have fellowship with Him, and walk in darkness, we lie, and do not the truth. But if we walk in the light, as He is in the light, we have fellowship one with another, and the blood of Jesus Christ His Son cleanseth us from all sin."

While "seasons of darkness" are not consistent with any degree of salvation it is well for us to distinguish between "darkness" and "heaviness." In 1 Pet. 1:5, 6, we read of a people "who are kept by the power of God through faith unto salvation ready to be revealed in the last time, wherein ye greatly rejoice, though now for a season, if need be, ye are in heaviness through manifold temptations." Sin brings darkness, while "manifold temptation" brings "heaviness." Unless the soul distinguishes between the two, it is in danger of making shipwreck of faith. For, be it remembered that Satan takes advantage of our moods. When a soul is suffering some temptations and consequent heaviness, Satan is most likely to whisper to that soul, "you don't feel as you once did, or as others say they feel," and then insinuates that "the probabilities are either you never had the blessing of sanctification or else that you have lost it." And having thus taken the attention and eye away from Jesus to yourself, and so started the wedge of doubt into your soul, he will whisper most adroitly. "You know you do not feel as you once did, and the probabilities are you have lost the blessing; at any rate, you do not want to be a hypocrite and profess what you do not have, and so you better say no more about sanctification until you feel different;" having listened to the devil, and having first given up your faith and now given up your testimony—all because you were in heaviness and did not feel as you desired—it is easy to see that defeat is inevitable. Many have lost their experience right at this point, simply because they did not understand that heaviness was consistent with holiness, and did not indicate the loss of divine favor. "Kept by the power of God," and "ready to be revealed in the last time," "though now for a season, if need be, ye are in heaviness, through manifold temptations."

The same persons of whom He said they had a "lively hope," and were "elect according to the fore-knowledge of God," and "ready to be revealed in the last time," are still subject to temptation and seasons of heaviness. The fact that there was heaviness did not indicate that they were not "kept."

It is well to remember that it is impossible for anyone always to feel just the same, and that God has never told us to feel, nor required any certain amount of feeling. It is not by our feeling but by our faith that we stand and honor God. Temptations will come, but temptation is not sin. We are told to "count it all joy when ye fall into divers temptations." If the devil is after you it proves he has not got you, and because of this you may well rejoice. Not only so, but the trial of your faith will mean the development and perfecting of your faith which will bring "a far more exceeding and eternal weight of glory," both in this world and the world to come!

THE WITNESS OF THE SPIRIT.

God does not purpose that we should be left in doubt and uncertainty relative to things pertaining to our eternal salvation. Hence we read, when a soul has truly repented and been regenerated by the HolyGhost, and adopted into the family of God, that, "The Spirit itself beareth witness with our spirit, that we are the children of God." (Rom. 8:16).

And just as certainly and distinctly as the "Spirit itself beareth witness with our spirit, that we are the children of God," so surely He in like manner bears witness to the subsequent work of Sanctification. We read in Hebrews 10:14-15, "For by one offering He hath perfected forever them that are sanctified, whereof the Holy Ghost also is a witness to us."

To what intent is the witness of the Spirit if it is not to give us positive assurance and knowledge of our relation to God. Hence none should take things for granted and assume and presume that they are in possession of grace to which the Spirit does not bear witness. This was the teaching of Mr. Wesley: "None, therefore ought to believe that the work is done till there is added the testimony of the Spirit witnessing his entire sanctification *as clearly as his justification."* (Plain Account p. 70.)

However, we would note that faith precedes, or rather is the condition of the witness of the Spirit. We cannot come into possession of either justification or sanctification until we believe for it; and we cannot exercise heart faith until we come on believing ground, where every scriptural requirement has been complied with. So the divine order is that we first meet the conditions—pay down the price—and having done this, which is our part, we now believe that according to His promise God does *now* perform and accomplish His part; and that when we thus come where the soul "believeth on the Son of God (for the blessing sought) he hath the witness in himself." That is, the instant faith really lays hold on the promise God sends a telegram from the skies by the Holy Ghost that the bank of Heaven has honored the draft and "counted" out to us the sum that faith had appropriated. The man or woman who has this certificate, bearing the witness and signature of the Holy Ghost, has no occasion to *"hope"* he has the blessing, nor will it matter much to him what any person may think or say about it, even though he be the preacher, presiding elder or bishop, seeing he has heard from heaven. He does not require visions nor the witness of men and angels, having heard from higher authority.

What constitutes the witness of the Spirit? This may be difficult to explain, seeing the Spirit has innumerable ways of bearing witness. In brief, the witness of the spirit is *the divine assurance, the voice of God in the soul,* that gives the conviction or knowledge to our inner consciousness, that the blessing sought is now mine. Many have supposed that it consisted in great ecstacies and rapturous joy; or a something in which one would experience a sensation similar to that which one might realize in taking hold of some galvanic battery. That there are cases where such manifestations are experienced we do not question. But it is nevertheless well to remember that the Holy Spirit can bear testimony to our inner consciousness without exciting our emotions. It may be just an unmistakable impression or conviction that will bring great quietude and restfulness; a divine enabling to appropriate and consciously rest on the Word of God.

It was the same Holy Spirit who came upon Jesus in the form of a dove, that came upon the desciples as "a rushing mighty wind." There is not much demonstration in a dove,—simply the gentle, subdued cooing. Perhaps we are safe in saying that the *manifestations* of the Spirit are rather the result of the *witness* of the spirit. We are not to seek any certain manifestation, but we are to believe God, and then the Holy Ghost will bear witness, and lift us out of the region of doubt and uncertainty into assurance, knowledge and victory. "It is the Spirit that beareth witness because the Spirit is truth. (1 John 5:6.)

"HIM" OR "IT."

Under the pretext of advanced spirituality, we sometimes hear men say, with a very significant shrug of the shoulders and shake of the head, it is not an "it" they want, or have, but "Him," meaning the Holy Spirit.

Now, all this sounds very nice, and to the unsophisticated, has the semblance of deep spirituality and superiority of experience; but the Bible student with experience and knowledge of the Satanic devices, and traits and tricks of the "old man," at once understands that in most instances such a speech is simply a "take off," and an evasive dodge gendered by a lack of spirituality and antipathy to a definite experience of heart purity obtained by entire sanctification. We have found that the carnal mind does not object to seeking a "deeper work of grace," or, "a baptism of power for service," or, "more of the Holy Spirit," so long as there is no insistence on the eradication and destruction of the sin-nature—the self-life.

In this same connection we hear it said, "it is not the blessing we want, but the Blesser." This is about equivalent to saying, "it is not the sunshine I want, but the sun;" or, "it is not water I want, but the fountain." But what is the sun for but to give forth sunshine; what is a fountain for but to give forth water; and what is a Blesser for but to bestow blessings? Even so "He"—the Holy Spirit—comes into the heart to do certain things in us and for us.

Paul was never beyond speaking of "blessings," and burst forth in thanksgiving for the same: "Blessed be the God and Father of our Lord Jesus Christ, who hath blessed us with all spiritual *blessings* in heavenly places (*things,* marg.) in Christ: according as He hath chosen us in Him before the foundation of the world, that we should be holy and without blame before Him in love." Eph. 1:3-4. In writing to the Romans he said, "I am sure that when I come unto you, I shall come in *the fullness of the blessing of the gospel of Christ.*" Rom. 15:29.

He also spoke of an "it," to "the church of the Thessalonians which is in God the Father and in the Lord Jesus Christ;" after praying in their behalf, "the very God of peace sanctify you wholly," he assured them, by saying, "faithful is He that calleth you, who also will do IT." 1 Thess., 5:23-24. In connection with the historic Pentecost we read, "And suddenly there came a sound from heaven as of a rushing mighty wind, and IT filled all the house where they were sitting. And there appeared unto them cloven tongues as of fire, and IT sat upon each of them." So we see there was an "it" in connection with the Pentecost, hence this term should not be very objectionable.

We would insist that before any one can have the Holy Spirit in His indwelling, abiding presence and pentecostal fullness, he must receive the "it" of sanctification,— that is, the cleansing of the heart from inbred sin. "Faithful is He that calleth you, who also will do it." If we would have the "Blesser" we must have the "blessings," to the end "that we should be holy." Well for us if we have "the fullness of the blessing of the gospel of Christ," then there will be no objection to "it," and no occasion or disposition to use evasive terms.

DIVINE GUIDANCE.

A truly consecrated soul will have no struggle about doing what it apprehends and knows clearly to be the will of God. If truly consecrated it was settled once for all that knowing the will of God, there must be unhesitating obedience. However, consecrated souls may at times have some difficulty in discerning clearly and knowing positively what is the will of God concerning some given matter. It is the purpose of the writer to suggest a few general principles whereby the soul may be able to "try the spirits whether they are of God," when there are conflicting voices.

First. Any leading or impression that may come should have a rigid comparison with the Word of God. The Spirit of God never leads any one contrary to the written

Word of God. The Spirit and the Word agree. When there is the least divergence from the spirit of the Word, or conflict with any passage of the letter of the Word of God, the leading or impression is from the devil.

Second. False spirits always plead personal and temporal interests, such as gain, or pleasure, or ease, or popularity, whereas the Spirit of God always pleads the glory of God, the salvation of souls and the rewards eternal. Asking the question as to where or how we may win the most souls, or best promote the glory of God will bring the answer to many perplexing problems.

Third. A false spirit will invariably *drive,* so that there is little or no time for meditation, deliberation and prayer, and the soul becomes confused, and chafed, and bewildered, and distressed, whereas Jesus invariably *leads* and inclines, and wooes, and draws the soul, by working in us, "both to will and to do of His good pleasure." Satan drives. "He brake the bands and was *driven of the devil.*" Jesus leads. "When He putteth forth his own sheep He goeth before them, and the sheep follow Him." Jesus leads, and there is always time for deliberation and prayer.

Fourth. The use of sanctified common sense. The soul truly and really led by the Spirit can not be charged with folly, as He never leads any one to any thing foolish, or contrary to good, sound, sanctified common sense. The gray matter in one's skull is for use. True, God may call a man to do that which is above or beyond human comprehension, so that the human mind may not understand the why and the wherefore, and men whose minds are darkened by sin may pronounce the act of obedience as foolish, nevertheless the vindication for the act will finally come, if in keeping with good sanctified common sense. We are supposed to use all the sense God has given us, and may rest assured that He will never direct to foolishness.

Fifth. Providential indications should ever be taken into account. The leadings of God and the providences of God will invariably harmonize.

If the Spirit of God leads a man to a certain work, along a given line, the hand of God by His providences, will open the door and open the way for the accomplishment of the same. God never leads a man to do the impossible. He will provide the means, and the way for the accomplishment of His own will and purpose. So there need be no throwing down of doors, upon our part, but simply the entering of the open door.

6. Entire consecration must ever be the attitude of the soul that would make no mistake, but discern plainly the will of God. When there is no pre-arranged plan or program, and no personal preference or choice but the will of God, the vision is undimmed and the voice of the Good Shepherd unmistakable.

"SINLESS PERFECTION."

"Sinless perfection" is a term used only by those who deny the possibility of any perfection. We are frequently asked, "Do you believe in sinless perfection?" Our answer is, "We never use that term, first, because it is an unscriptural term, and, second, because it is an ambiguous term. It all depends on what is meant by the term "sinless perfection.' "

In asking the question, "Do you believe in sinless perfection," they usually mean to say, "Do you believe in becoming so good and holy you could not sin if you wanted to?" We answer, if this is meant, "No, we do not believe in 'sinless perfection.'"

But if by "sinless perfection" is meant a salvation that saves men perfectly from all sin, we would answer in the affirmative, and insist that the Bible teaches that sort of "sinless perfection." We insist that if Jesus Christ can save a man from any sin, He can save Him from *all* sin. This is the promise, "If we walk in the light . . . the blood of Jesus Christ His Son cleanseth us from all sin." 1 John 1:7.

While we do not teach or believe any man can become so good and holy he could not *sin if he wanted to,* we do believe and teach that men may be so thoroughly saved they will not want to, and by the grace of God, do not commit sin. We do not say, we have not power to sin, yet all may know of an experience where thew have power not to commit sin. "He that committeth sin is of the devil. . . . Whosoever is born of God doth not commit sin."

Perfection, as applied to religious experience has to do with quality rather than quantity. We must ever distinguish between purity and maturity. A child may be just as perfect as a child as an adult is perfect as an adult. If Satan can make a man a perfect sinner, then Jesus Christ can make a man a perfect Christian.

Perfection is not a human attainment. It is not something we do, so much as something God does for us.

The only perfection we may hope to reach is *the perfection of love.* That is the perfection enjoined in Matt. 5:48.

All Christians have love, but all Christians do not have *perfect* love. "Perfect love casteth out fear: because fear hath torment. He that feareth is not *made* perfect in love."

Who then is a perfect Christian? He whose heart is cleansed from all sin, and filled with pure, unmixed love, so that he loves God with all his heart, and his neighbor as himself. Three tests of perfect love may be found as follows:

Obedience to the Word, I John 2:5; Love one to another, I John 4:12; Freedom from tormenting fear, I John 4:17, 18.

"FIRST PURE, THEN PEACEABLE."

HOLINESS is not only freedom from sin, but means antagonism to sin. God not only saves men from sin, who will repent and walk in the light, but is unalterably opposed to sin, and will punish all who resist and continue to sin. To be at peace with sin is to be at variance with God, and to cry "Peace, peace, when there is no peace." (Jer. 8:11.) Hence we read "That the friendship of the world is enmity with God; whosoever, therefore, will be a friend of the world is the enemy of God." (Jas. 4:4.) The attitude of silent acquiescence is the spirit of compromise. While Jesus says to His blood-washed disciple, "Peace I leave with you, my peace I give unto you." John 14:27; He also says, "Think not that I am come to send peace on earth: I came not to send peace, but a sword." (Matt. 10:34.)

The purified soul is at peace and in harmony with everything that is pure, but must wage an unrelenting warfare against everything that is evil. The same passage containing the injunction to "Preach the Word," says, "Reprove, rebuke." (2 Tim. 4:2.) "Them that sin rebuke before all, that others also may fear." (1 Tim. 5: 20.) "Cry aloud, spare not, lift up thy voice like a trumpet, and shew my people their transgressions, and the house of Jacob their sins." Isa. 58:1. Whosoever does this will incur the displeasure of those who are unwilling to forsake sin, and will be regarded as a disturber of the peace, creating dissension and strife. "They hate him that rebuketh in the gate, and they abhor him that speaketh uprightly." Amos 5:10.

It is frequently urged that the preaching of holiness causes division in the church—and so it does—and rightly so. Men who do not want purity and holiness want sin. There is nothing else to want. And "he that committeth sin is of the devil." 1 John 3:8. However, the preaching of holiness does not create the division; it simply reveals the division that already exists—and must forever exist—between the lovers of purity and the lovers of impurity. Such a division is scriptural, and essential to the real progress of the work of God. The Apostle Paul encouraged this division, when, referring to the "lovers of pleasure having a form of godliness but denying the power," he said "from such turn away," 2 Tim. 3:4-5. "If there come any unto you, and bring not this doctrine, receive him not into your house, neither bid him God speed; for he that biddeth him God speed is a partaker of his evil deeds," 2 John 10:11. It is just as much a religious duty to frown at evil as to rejoice in the truth. Because Eli "frowned not" (marg. I Sam., 3:13) upon his sons when they did evil, the wrath of God came upon him. Before there can be scriptural peace there must be purity. The preaching of sanctification does not divide pure people, it unites them. Jesus prayed "sanctify them that they all may be one," John 17:17-21. Not holiness, but the lack of holiness, is the source of division.

"Be ye not unequally yoked together with, unbelievers; for what fellowship hath righteousness with unrighteousness? and what communion hath, light with, darkness? And what concord hath, Christ with Belial? or what part hath he that believeth with an infidel? . . . Wherefore come out from among them and be ye separate," 2 Cor. 6:14:17. "Ye that love the Lord hate evil," Ps. 97:10. At peace with everybody and everything that is pure; but while we love the sinner we must be in arms and arrayed against all that is evil. "First pure then peaceable."

PERFECTION AND GROWTH.

The perfection enjoined by scripture and possible for all Christians, is the perfection of a heart cleansed from all sin and filled with pure love—*the perfection of love.*

The term, perfection, has reference to quality rather than quantity.

We have met those who objected to Christian perfection on the grounds that if one were perfect, it would exclude the possibility of growth and development in grace. It is urged by such, that if one were perfect there could be neither necessity nor opportunity for growth. Such need only be reminded that Christian perfection refers to the *quality* rather than the *quantity* of love in the heart. All

Christians have love; but all Christians have not *perfect* love, which casteth out fear.

What perfect health is to the body, perfect love is to the soul. Holiness means spiritual wholeness, or, soul health. Sin is a malady, a disease, and is always an abnormal condition.

Because a child enjoys perfect health is no reason why it may not continue to grow; the facts are, perfect health is the condition for growth. The child with perfect health will grow far more rapidly and symmetrically than will the child with impaired health.

We need ever bear in mind, that it is not *perfection of action,* but *perfect love,* which has respect mainly to *kind* or *quality*, we are contending for. In the language of the Rev. J. A. Wood, in "Purity and Maturity" we insist: "A thing may be said to be perfect when it possesses all the properties or qualities which are essential to its nature. The fruit of the Spirit is perfect when it exists in the soul in exclusion of every opposing principle, every contrary temper—perfect in quality."

As already intimated, growth in grace will be more rapid when the heart is cleansed from all sin and perfected in love, than it otherwise could be. One of the essentials to growth is knowledge. We can never love a person of whom we have no knowledge. In proportion as our knowledge extends, in that proportion have we an intellectual basis for the action of love.

"Accordingly, every new manifestation of God's character, every new exhibition of His attributes, every additional development of his providences will furnish new occasions for love. It is the privilege, therefore, of a person perfected in love, and consequently a holy person, to increase in holiness in exact proportion with his increase in knowledge." (Upham."

When a heart is cleansed from *all* sin it can not be made any more pure, but there may be an unceasing increase of pure love in a purified heart. There can be no growing into perfect love, since growth does not change the quality or nature of any thing, but there may be unstinted and illimitable growth in grace when love is perfected in the heart.

WHY MEN OPPOSE HOLINESS.

First.—Because they love sin and are not willing to give it up and turn from it. When a man is done with sin he wants holiness. There is nothing else to want. He who does not believe in holiness must believe in sin. We have found that the objections to holiness are more frequently the outcome of moral conditions than of mental difficulties. Certainly, the moral condition gives color to the eye. "Unto the pure all things are pure: but unto them that are defiled and unbelieving is nothing pure; but even their mind and conscience is defiled." A man with a pure heart can see purity everywhere, while a man with sin in his heart can see purity nowhere. Our likes and dislikes are controlled largely by our appetency—the things we long for and desire; and our desires are determined by the condition or nature ruling within. A turkey buzzard will alight upon a carcass, because such is the nature and desire of the bird; whereas, a humming bird will just as naturally alight in a flower garden, because that is the nature and desire of the humming bird. The more we are partakers of the divine nature the more intense our love and desire for holiness.

Second.—Men oppose holiness because of their ignorance concerning the Scriptures and the power of God. As Jesus said to the Pharisee: "Ye do err, not knowing the Scriptures, nor the power of God." Any person antagonizing holiness does one of two things: either he publishes his *ignorance* or his *infidelity* concerning the Bible. The terms "holy" and "holiness" occur more than six hundred times in the Bible, and are frequently applied to human characters under the operations of grace. If Jesus Christ can save a man from any sin, He can save him from all sin. Being ignorant concerning the real Bible teachings on this subject of holiness accounts for much of the prejudice and opposition concerning it. The facts are, the subject of holiness is so Scriptural, reasonable and logical that no one can antagonize it without first mis-stating and misrepresenting the matter.

Third.—In the last analysis, opposition to holiness is due to the "carnal mind' in the hearts of men, which, "is enmity against God; for it is not subject to the law of God, neither indeed can be." This "enmity" is innate and inborn, and is not only at *enmity,* but is within itself the very quintessence of "enmity against God." In another place it is called, "our old man." In opposing holiness this "old man" is actuated by the devil, and is simply fighting for his own life; holiness means death to the "old man." The "carnal mind" is a condition—a principle— within, which cannot be pardoned, but must be eradicated and destroyed by the blood of Jesus. So wherever opposition to the blood of Jesus manifests itself, that very opposition is in itself the strongest evidence of the lack and need of holiness. The opposition proves that the principle of *"enmity"* is still in the heart.

He who does not want holiness wants *"unholiness,"* or sin, no matter what his profession or pretentions may be. All men realize the fact that holiness is necessary for entering heaven—and so, theoretically, all men want holiness at the end of life; but to desire holiness only at death, is not to desire it at all. If there is a real desire for holiness, it must be in the present tense; and if holiness is desired in the present tense, why should there be any objection to a present tense experience of holiness?

How any person can profess to love God, who is the very essence and embodiment of holiness, and yet be antagonistic to holiness, is indeed a mystery. Or. how a man can believe God is holy, and not want to be like Him, is difficult to understand. "Every man that hath this hope in him (the hope of seeing Jesus as He is) purifieth himself, *even as He is pure.*" I Jno., 3:3.

Many will admit of a *relative* holiness, but deny the possibility of a *positive* holiness. To strive to be holier than in former days, does not seem objectionable, but to insist on being positively cleansed from ALL sin seems to them a very dangerous heresy. But to deny the possibility of being thus cleansed is to doubt the efficacy of the blood of Christ and deny the Scripture. A heart in which there remains any sin surely is not holy. The holiness commanded, and enjoined upon us, is: "AS He which hath called you is holy, SO be ye holy." "*As*"—"*So*," would seem to indicate that the heart is to be positively clean. To demand a holy life, and yet deny me the privilege of a holy heart is demanding the impossible. "Thou blind Pharisee cleanse *first* that which is within the cup and platter, that the outside of them may be clean also."

By holiness is meant, a heart cleansed from all sin, and filled with pure love, so as to love God with all the heart and our neighbor as ourselves. There is surely nothing objectionable about an experience like that. A holy God inspired holy men by the Holy Ghost to write a holy Bible to tell us that Christ died to make us holy, and that we must be holy in order to enter a holy heaven and associate with holy angels and dwelll with a holy God.

DEFINITENESS.

The importance of being specific and definite can scarcely be exaggerated. A preacher may preach on repentance or the new birth in an indefinite way for a whole year, and no one will be awakened or converted. In like manner he may preach *about* sanctification and holiness in an indefinite way, and no one will be offended and no one will seek and obtain the experience. This is the difficulty with much of the preaching of these days; it is all of the sheet-lightning sort, and strikes nowhere. God's truth will not return void, and if preached explicitly, specifically, and definitely will invariably precipitate a revival along the lines of truth thus emphasized. A preacher who aims at nothing definite, and deals simply in glittering generalities should not be disappointed if his ministry is unfruitful. Much of the preaching of these days reminds one of the dudish preacher, who had some convictions of truth, but feared that by being too definite and specific he might offend his congregation, and hence endeavored to round the corners by saying, "You are all sinners,—*so to speak;* unless you repent—*to a certain extent;* and be converted—*to a certain degree,* you will all be damned—*in a certain measure.*" Of course no one is offended and no one is helped.

Holiness will not win and prosper where men generalize either in sermon or testimony. Presumably all preachers think they are lifting up the standard of holiness,—and indeed many of them do preach some good doctrine—but neutralize it all by apologizing and generalizing before they finish, and no one gets the experience. Of course it is difficult to preach an experience and lead others into an experience that one does not himself enjoy. We venture the assertion that any preacher who is called of God, who will himself seek and obtain the experience of sanctification, and will then explicitly and definitely preach it, and bear definite testimony, can have a revival almost any time and anywhere. When not willing to do this, he must content himself with failure, so far as soul saving is concerned, and let himself down easy by saying, "the people are Gospel-hardened," or, "conditions and circumstances were unfavorable." As Mr. Wesley observed, concerning the failure of certain Methodist preachers on Launceston Circuit, "either they did not speak of perfection at all (the peculiar doctrine committed to our trust) or they speak of it *only in general terms,* without urging the believers to go on unto perfection, and to expect it every moment. And *wherever this is not done* the work of God does not prosper." (Vol. 4, p. 459.)

This same principle obtains in seeking God. A person may pray for pardon in an indefinite, round-about way for forty years and never get it; but finally he becomes desperate and strikes out across lots, definitely asking God to forgive his sins, and is soon the glad recipient of the grace he sought. In like manner a Christian may pray in a vague indefinite manner, "create within me a clean heart," "give me more religion," etc., etc., and never get it. Finally in the desperation of his soul, he cries out definitely, "sanctify me wholly," "take inbred sin out of my heart," "deliver me from the carnality of my heart," etc., and soon obtains the blessed experience of entire sanctification. Whenever a soul is definite with God, God will be pleased to be definite with that soul.

Jesus taught us this when He said, "if a son shall ask bread of any of you that is a father, will he give him a stone? or if he ask a fish will he for a fish give him a serpent? or if he ask for an egg, will he offer him a scorpion?" The thought is that we should ask definitely for what we want, and then expect to receive exactly what we have asked for. Be definite in preaching, in prayer, and in testimony and a definite work will be accomplished. Amen.

CONSECRATION AND SANCTIFICATION.

Consecration is not entire sanctification. Consecration is a human act, whereas sanctification is a divine act. Consecration is what you must do in order that God may sanctify you wholly.

Many have confounded consecration with surrender, and so insisted that they consecrated all and were wholly sanctified when converted. This is unscriptural and unreasonable. We ever need to remember that our attitude toward God, as sinners, was that of a rebel—rebelling against the government of heaven; and as rebels we could simply surrender, and take the oath of allegiance to heaven's king. This surrender was made because of the fear of the results and penalties of sin, and because Jesus had conquered us. With many of us conviction for sin became so intense we were literally compelled to surrender or consent to be damned. Not so in consecration. Consecration is rather the glad, free-will offering of our all, including ourselves, to Jesus because of the love in our hearts for Him; the constraint of love.

The penitent sinner surrenders that which is evil in order that Jesus may receive and forgive him; the child of God consecrates himself and his all that is good in order that God may purify and use him.

Nowhere in scripture is a sinner exhorted to consecrate; nor has he anything to consecrate. But in writing to Christians, the Apostle says, "I beseech you, therefore, brethren, by the mercies of God, that ye present your bodies a living sacrifice, holy, acceptable unto God, which is your reasonable service." As sinners we were "dead in trespasses and sins," and therefore could not present ourselves "a living sacrifice" until after we were "quickened" by the Holy Spirit. This exhortation is to the *"brethren."* Why should they be urged to thus present themselves if they had already done so, at the time of their conversion? Not the judgments of God, and the wrath to come, but " the mercies of God" are urged as the reason for this consecration. If this offering of ourselves to God is but "our reasonable service" then anything short of this must be unreasonable.

We have no sympathy with modern consecration meetings which call every two weeks for the re-consecration of ourselves to God. We might as consistently urge that people should be re-married every two weeks. Consecration means the solemn devotement and deeding over to God ourselves and all that pertains to us—all we know and all we don't know—for time and eternity. Where such an agreement is once entered upon, there remains nothing to consecrate, and certainly nothing to *reconsecrate,* while time lasts. After all is given to God it no longer belongs to us. The term re-consecrate would indicate that we had taken something back; such an act would be stealing, and would require repentance. After a consecration is made, which comprehends all, for time and eternity, it may nevertheless be a pleasure at times to walk about the altar and look up into the face of Jesus and tell Him you mean it more than ever, and so intensify your consecration.

As in the case of Abraham and Elijah, when the sacrifice is complete upon the altar of God, the fire will fall. There is no occasion to sing,

"I'm waiting for the fire."

The faithfulness of God and the present tense of every promise is the guarantee of a present tense work. Let there be definiteness in the consecration—consecration for the purpose of being made holy—and we will still find that, "Whatsoever toucheth the altar shall be holy." Consecrate not to a work, or cause, but to God, and then trust Him to sanctify you wholly.

SANCTIFICATION AND PERSONALITY.

Sanctification does not destroy our individuality or peculiar traits of personality. It simply destroys inbred sin out of the heart. The facts are, that by delivering the soul from the bondage of fear touching the opinions and criticisms of men, and from the grave-clothes of carnality, it bounds into liberty, and hence more fully asserts and manifests the real personality of the individual. Sanctification brings people down from their stilts, and putting on of airs and takes away all the strut and swagger and makes them act natural. It gives to men a sort of supernatural naturalness.

Much of the ordinary religious exercises are wholly unnatural, because of the unnatural tones of the voice, the strained attitudes, affectations, and the fear that some one might criticise, and the desire to make a favorable impression. There are those who can speak fluently on almost any subject, but when they come to speak in a religious service they can only repeat some little stereotyped statement; others, who are naturally demonstrative, rather than be regarded as enthusiasts, will quench and grieve the Spirit, by poking a handkerchief into the mouth, etc., all of which is unnatural.

One of the beauties of sanctification is that it makes people "free indeed," and without having their thoughts fixed upon themselves they are simply passive and pliable in the hands of the Holy Ghost.

While we believe that "the spirits of the prophets are subject to the prophets," (I Cor. 14:32), and therefore may not plead for demonstrations which would do injury either to the bodies of men, or destroying furniture, etc., indulging in all sorts of antics and contortions, yet we must accord to men the utmost liberty in the Holy Ghost, to manifest, according to their own personality, the Spirit and power of God in their own hearts.

God evidently loves variety in nature and so, doubtless, does in the kingdom of grace. He certainly does not want His children to ape and mimic each other. Some one has said, there are many kinds of "tators," but the worst kind of "tators" are the imi-tators. We have seen where a church, or, indeed, an entire denomination took on certain tones of voice and forms of expression, imitating certain whines, and shouts, until you could tell the instant you heard them speak, just what creed they had subscribed to. The whole thing was unnatural, unscriptural, and without excuse.

God has given to every man a distinct personality, and those distinguishing marks of personality may be branded by others as eccentricities, oddities and singularities, but under the sanctifying power and blessing of God may become a source of strength and gloriously effective for God.

To be just as natural and free in a religious service as one would be anywhere else, is surely the privilege of every Christian. If God had wanted us to be like some one else, He would undoubtedly have made us so. He never intended that the layman should imitate the class-leader; and the class-leader the local preacher, and the local preacher imitate the pastor; and the pastor imitate the presiding elder; and the presiding elder imitate the bishop or college president, etc. If He has called you to a certain work it is evident the Lord needed and wanted a person just like you, hence has chosen you. So let Him sanctify you and enable you to be perfectly natural—to be real to yourself—in the Holy Ghost.

Amen.

WHY THE PREACHING OF HOLINESS IS ESSENTIAL TO REVIVALS.

FIRST: The preaching of holiness is essential because holiness is the divine standard which God would have us lift up. He who does not believe in holiness must believe in sin. To deny the possibility of holiness in this life is equivalent to saying Jesus can not save from all sin. Men must understand that in order to be saved at all they must abandon and forsake all sin. Even sinners recognize that a "sinning religion" does not commend itself, and admit that holiness is the true standard. They naturally and most truthfully reason concerning professors of religion who insist they cannot live without sin, that they are just as good as those professors, since they are both living the same way.

SECOND. The definite preaching of holiness is always strengthening and stimulating to those who are Christians, as it edifies them, and brings them to see their need and privileges, and so stirs them up to more diligent heart-searchings and consequent calling upon God. Thus the revival begins where a true revival must always begin. Whenever the children of God get out into the tides of full salvation, and hence have the joys of salvation, and are free and impelled to service by the fullness of the Spirit, sinners invariably come under conviction, and begin to seek God. Jesus said, in speaking of His disciples, concerning the Holy Spirit, "And when he is come (to you who are Christians) He will reprove the world of sin and of righteousness." Generally speaking, Christians lack the fullness of the Spirit and consequently there is no conviction. The Holy Spirit does the work of conviciton most generally through the *overflow* of Christian hearts.

THIRD. The preaching of holiness is essential that by contrast sinners may see their distance from God. A man may never realize his poverty until he stands by the side of some multi-millionaire; or how ignorant he is, until he comes in contact with those who are far advanced along intellectual lines, and are greatly his superiors; just so a man may never realize how sinful he is until he has a glimpse of God's holiness. It was when Isaiah had a vision of the holiness of God that he began to cry out, "I am undone." So in magnifying the holiness of God men will come to more fully realize the necessity of being holy if they would dwell with a holy God. If God is holy, I must be holy.

FOURTH. Then, again, the definite preaching of holiness at once clearly draws the lines of battle, for there is nothing that the devil so much hates, and God so much delights to bless, as the definite preaching of holiness. The preaching of holiness causes agitation, and when men become aroused and agitated they will give attention and begin to think, and when they begin to think, the Holy Spirit has special opportunity. Where there is no agitation there is invariably stagnation. As intimated, God will always bless the uncompromising preaching of holiness. But some one will inquire, would you preach holiness to sinners? I would answer, "yes," and then teach them that in order to reach holiness they must first repent and be born again. When God sent Moses into Egypt He did not tell him to preach to them about, or start them for the wilderness of Zin, but started them at once for Canaan, though it required two crossings to reach Canaan.

The objective point of all the provisions of the atonement, and of every commandment and promise in the Bible, is holiness. He "hath blessed us with all spiritual blessings in heavenly things (marg.) in Christ ACCORDING as he hath chosen us in him before the foundation of the world, *that we should be holy* and without blame before him in love." Eph. 1:3, 4. "Holiness, without which no man shall see the Lord." Heb. 12:14.

SOME QUESTIONS ANSWERED.

First. If perfect, how could there be any more growth in grace?"

This is a question often asked whenever the doctrine of Christian perfection is proclaimed. It need be remembered that Christian perfection has reference to quality rather than quantity. What perfect health would be to the body, perfect love, heart purity, sanctification and holiness is to the soul. Sin is a disease. Holiness which is the condition or state in which love is perfected, implying perfect soul health, is recovery from the malady or disease of sin.

A child may enjoy just as perfect health and be just as perfect as a child as an adult enjoys perfect health, and is perfect as an adult. And the fact that the child enjoys perfect health—freedom from all disease—is no reason why it may not continue to grow until it reaches manhood or womanhood. Indeed perfect health is the condition for rapid and symmetrical development and growth. Every one knows that a child in perfect health grows more rapidly than a child that is sickly and diseased. Certain it is when a heart is cleansed from all sin and filled with pure and perfect love, it cannot be made any more pure, but it may enlarge and obtain more perfect love and then it may go on and enlarge some more and obtain some more perfect love; and then it may enlarge some more and go on and obtain some more perfect love and thus it may continue *ad infinitum.* Amen and amen!

Second. If the carnal nature were all destroyed and the heart made perfectly pure and holy, cleansed from all inbred sin, how could a person sin again?

This question is frequently asked with great seriousness, as though indeed it would be a great calamity should one become so thoroughly saved he could not sin any more. When one talks thus it looks a little suspicious or at least awakens the suspicion that such an one is not quite done with sin, and so desires license or liberty to indulge in sin occasionally. Thank God there are some people who are forever done with sin, and have gone entirely out of the sin business. They would still believe in holiness even if they knew that would fix them so they could never sin again. They would be perfectly ready to say, "Good Lord if it is possible to fix me so I can never sin again, fix me quickly." It certainly would be no very great misfortune to be thus "fixed."

But the question may be answered by asking another question: "How could Adam and Eve, who were created 'in the image of God' and so had no sin-ward bent, but were in the 'likeness' of God—how could they commit sin?" or "How could angels, who surely have no inbred sin, but are pure and holy, commit sin?" Surely not because there were roots of sin, or sinward tendencies in their hearts. Free agency carries with it the power of choice. Sin is presented from without and in the exercise of his free agency a man can choose good or evil. "But why should he choose the evil if there is no appetite for sin in his heart?" It is well to remember that Satan does not present sin as sin, but rather as something "to be desired to make one wise" etc, and says, even though you do partake, "ye shall not surely die." Temptation appeals to the will, and when the will yields and consents to the temptation, sin enters. Holiness does not deprive one of the use of his volition;

if it did man would simply be a machine. The right attitude of the will in an eternal "yes" to God—is essential to the maintenance of holiness of heart.

Third. "If, the 'old man is crucified,' and all inbred sin is cleansed out of the heart, how can the 'old man' again revive, or sin enter the heart?"

This question, too, may be answered by asking another question: "how did it first enter into Adam and Eve?" It doubtless would enter into our hearts in the same way. As intimated in the answer to the question above, the will is the gateway to the city of man-soul. Sin is not a material substance in the heart, though it is a very definite reality. Sin is often the mis-use and perversion of that which is God-given and so is perfectly right and legitimate within itself. When the human will unites and agrees with the suggestion and will of Satan, sin is conceived, and there is instantly a sinful state and condition, even though there has been no overt act of sin. One might as well ask how disease could enter a perfectly healthy body; the answer would be, by the perversion of some law of nature. As with a healthy body, so with a healthy or holy soul; with this difference, that sickness and disease may come into the body without the consent of the will. As a diseased condition of the body gives a predisposition and therefore a greater liability to other attacks of disease; so where sin is in the heart there is a greater susceptibility and danger to sin. Perfect soul-health is the safest and best condition for resisting and overcoming the disease without.

THE WILL OF GOD.

To the obedient child the will of the parent is law, and to the truly consecrated child of God the will of God— either as revealed in His Word or by His Spirit—is the rule for life and practice. Just in proportion as the human will embraces the will of God just in that proportion can the individual know true rest of soul, and fellowship with God. And our surrender and obedience to the will of God is the measure of our love to God and faith in God. It is folly for a man to profess that he loves God, and yet be in rebellion against the revealed will of God. Jesus taught, "If a man love me, he will keep my words." "He that hath my commandments, and keepeth them, he it is that loveth me." The commandments of God are simply the revealed and expressed will of God. No man can be a Christian and be indifferent concerning the will of God.

"If any man will do his will he shall know of the doctrine." So we see it is not mental difficulties but heart difficulties— an unwillingness to do the will of God—that hinders one from experiencing and understanding "the doctrine" expressing the will of God. "This is the will of God, even your sanctification." Many regard the doctrine of sanctification as though it were simply the dogma of some church or the theory of some zealots and religious enthusiasts; but the Bible says plainly *"this is the will of God*—EVEN YOUR—SANCTIFICATION." (1 Thess. 4:3.) If sanctification is the will of God concerning us, then we should never be content until we know definitely and positively that the will of God, even our sanctification, is accomplished in us. Sanctification being the will of God concerning us, no one is what God wills and desires him to be until sanctified.

Not only is sanctification the will of God, but we read, (Eph. 5:25-27) "Christ also loved the Church, and gave Himself for it, that He might sanctify and cleanse it." "Wherefore Jesus also, that He might sanctify the people with His own blood, suffered without the gate." From these passages we learn, *first,* that Jesus died in order to make our sanctification a possibility, thus enabliing us to have the will of God accomplished in us. *Second,* we learn that sanctification is for "the Church," which is made up of God's children—only true believers; that sanctification is a *second* experience, being for those who already have been converted, and so constitute "the Church." *Third,* we learn that sanctification is a divine act—something that Jesus must do in us—and therefore cannot be attained by growth, or death, or religious activities, or purgatory, but that Jesus does the work of sanctifying, "with His own blood." We can never grow into something He must do for us. *"Sanctified by faith."* (Acts 26:18.)

To resist and reject "the will of God" is disobedience, and disobedience is sin, and sin brings guilt and condemnation and spiritual death. Hence, the person that refuses or neglects sanctification, because of his disobedience, is in danger of losing his soul. True happiness can only be known to those who abide in the center of God's will.

ALONE WITH JESUS.

"And when they were alone, He expounded all things to His disciples."—Mark 4:34.

The disciple who would have the explanation, interpretation and unfolding of the scriptures must tarry alone with Jesus. Secrets are not divulged while surrounded by the multitudes, and while busily engaged and pre-occupied. If you would confide in a friend and really open up your heart you wait until such a time as your friend is disengaged and can take time to come apart and be alone with you. So they who would know the secret and hidden things of God and have Him "expound all things," must find time and opportunity to be alone with Him.

Such is the philosophy of love; while there may be the throbbing heart, and some expressions of affection in the presence of the multitudes, the hour of true bliss is that when the doors are closed, the curtains drawn, or, in the secluded nook or corner, the lovers are left alone. It is there that love finds her opportunity for expression, and the confiding heart gives forth its secrets. The intensity of love demands the secret interview and longs for an opportunity of being alone with the object of its love.

We read of "the secret place of the Most High" (Ps. 91:1), and "the secret of the Lord is with them that fear Him" (Ps. 25:14). So we can see plainly the Lord has secrets and a secret place for His children. How beautiful it is to feel and know that one is permitted to come into "the secret place of the Most High." Visitors and strangers come into reception halls and parlors, but only they who are in most intimate relations—known to be tried and true—can come into the secret place; and what is the meaning of a secret place, but the shutting out of all that might intrude or detract; to be left alone with the object of its love? Again we say, the deepest expressions of mutual affection, confidence and pleasure are not in public assemblies, in hurried greetings and mere social relations, but in the "secret place," alone and unobserved. It is then, and then only, that the most sacred things are mentioned and deepest secrets confided. It is exactly so in our relations to Jesus. Men and women who fail to take time to be much "alone" in the "secret place" with Jesus, are never deeply spiritual and are compelled to get their news concerning the kingdom second-handed. They know simply what the preacher or some one else tells them; hence, they are ever running after men—the newest preacher and the latest evangelist—to get some more news, second-handed, concerning the King's business. But they who have learned the secret of being much alone with Him in the secret place, get the secrets of the Lord directly from the King himself, and so are not dependent on the newspapers for the latest news. It is a wonderful thing that Jesus should take us into His confidence, and tell us the very secrets of His own loving heart. Not to the multitude, but to those who tarried alone with Him, did "He expound all things."

No amount of religious activities or service can make up for the lack of secret communion and fellowship with God. Joseph and Mary had been engaged in the worship and service of the Temple when they lost Jesus, and traveled a whole day's journey "supposing Him to have been in the company" before they discovered they had lost Him. One may become so absorbed with religious work and duties—so hurried and pre-occupied—that there is no time for secret prayer, and being alone with Him and the Word, and become lean in soul and backslide while thus engaged in the work of the Temple.

TRIALS.

The way we act under trial shows what we are.

Trials and temptations are to Christians what the weights on the old fashioned clocks were—kept them going.

Trials and temptations prove the measure of our moral strength. No man is stronger than his weakest point, even as a chain is no stronger than its weakest link.

As the eagle teaches her young to fly by tearing up the nest, and tossing the little birdlings into the air, thus compelling them to strike out their little spurs of wings, even so God teaches us the life of faith by way of persecution, adversity and trial.

As the damming up of the stream is the secret of increased force and power, so the trial of faith, means increased power and usefulness by giving a stronger grip on God in the development of our graces.

As the ancient Parthians believed that the strength of every foe they conquered entered into their own bodies, so we may gather from every temptation added strength and power. "Each victory will help us another to win." The time when God proves us is the challenge for us to prove Him. We need to remember that God has placed a "hedge" about His people, as Satan himself had to confess in the case of Job, (1:10) and Satan can not touch us until he has permission from God. So instead of censuring men, or even going on a tirade against Satan, we should accept all the trials of life, which are beyond our control, as in the permissive providence of God. Nothing can touch His child until it has first passed through the Father's hands for inspection.

"From vintages of sorrow are deepest joys distilled;
And the cup outstretched for healing is oft at Marah filled.
God leads to joy through weeping, to quietness through strife;
Through yielding into conquest; through death to endless life.
Be still, He hath enrolled thee, for the kingdom and the crown.
Be silent, let Him mould thee, who calleth thee His own."

BIBLE READINGS.

CHRISTIAN PERFECTION.

Required.
Matt. 5:48.
2 Cor. 13:11.
Heb. 6:1.
Gen. 17:1.

Prayed for.
Heb. 13:21.
Col. 4:12.
II Cor. 13:9.

Provided.
Heb. 7:19.
II Tim. 3:17.
Eph. 4:12, 13.
Matt. 19:21.

Experienced.
Gen. 6:9.
Job. 1:1.
Phil. 3:15.
I John 4:17, 18.
Heb. 10:14.
Jas. 1:4.

Miscellaneous.

Ps. 37:37; Isa. 26:3; John 17:23; I Cor. 2:6; Col. 1:28; James 3:2; Col. 3:14.

HEART PURITY.

Required.
Matt. 5:8.
I Tim. 1:5.
I Tim. 5:22.

Experienced.
I Pet. 1:22.
Acts 15:8, 9.
Psa. 24:4.

Provided.
Titus 2:14.
I John 3:3.
Heb. 9:13, 14.

Miscellaneous.
Titus 1:15.
I Tim. 4:12.
Jas. 4:8.

SANCTIFICATION.

Required.
I Thess. 4:3.
Lev. 20:7.
Heb. 12:14 (R. V.)

Provided.
Heb. 13:12.
Eph. 5:25, 27.
John, 17:19.

Prayed for.
John 17:17.
I Thess. 5:23.
Acts 20:32.

Experienced.
Jude 1:1.
Heb. 2:11.
I Pet. 1:2.

Miscellaneous.

2 Thess. 2:13; Rom. 15:16! Acts 26:18; 1 Cor. 6:11; II Tim. 2:21; Heb. 10:10; Matt. 23:19.

HOLINESS.

Required.
I Pet. 1:15; 16.
I Thess. 4:7.
Heb. 12:14.
II Cor. 7:1.

Provided.
Luke 1:73-75.
Heb. 10:19.
Eph. 4:24.
Eph. 5:27.
Col. 1:22.

Promised.
Eph. 1: 3, 4.
I Pet. 2:9.
Isa. 35:8.
2 Tim. 1:9.

Experienced.
2 Pet. 1:21.
I Pet. 3:5.
Heb. 3:1.
I Thess. 5:27.

Miscellaneous.

I Thess. 3:13; Tit. 1:8; I Cor. 3:17; Rom. 6:22; Rev. 22:11; I Thess. 2:10; Heb 12:10

PASSAGES OF SCRIPTURE SUGGESTING THE TWO EXPERIENCES.

"Pardon iniquities;" "Cleanse iniquity." Jer. 33:8.

"Blot out transgressions—in the plural; Wash and cleanse from iniquity and sin—in the singular. Ps. 51:1, 2.

"An highway *and* a way." Isa. 35:8.

"After that He put his hands again upon his eyes." Two touches necessary before he could see clearly. Mark 8:22-25.

"Righteousness *and* sanctification." I Cor. 1:30.

Engrafting and so becoming a "branch"—having life and fruit—one experience; After there is fruit, the promise of a purging and cleansing, and more fruit, a second experience. John 15:2.

Deliverance from "Condemnation," one experience; deliverance from "the law of sin and death," a second experience. Rom. 8:1,2.

"Justified by faith, we have peace with God," one experience; "Also we have access by faith into this grace wherein we stand," and glory in tribulations also. Rom. 5:1, 2. Another experience.

"Redeem us from all iniquity *and* purify." Titus 2:14.

Becoming the sons of God and having the hope of seeing him as he is, one experience; after this, "purifieth himself even as He is pure," a second experience. I John 3:1-3.

To forgive us our sins *and* to cleanse. I John, 1:7-9.

"Cleanse your hands, ye sinners;" a sinner is one who commits sin; "and purify your hearts ye double minded." A double-minded man is a man with two minds—the carnal mind and the mind of the Spirit. Jas. 4:8.

"Christ also loved the church and gave Himself for it that He might sanctify and cleanse it." Sanctification is for the church not for sinners. *"The Church"* is made up of all true believers. It is one experience to be born into "the church," and only after that do we become eligible to the sanctifying grace. Eph. 5:25-27.

"I indeed baptize you with water unto repentance," which brought to them the remission of sins, (Luke 3:3); "He shall baptize you with the Holy Ghost and fire," Mat. 3:11. The baptism with the Holy Ghost is given to believers only, John 14:17, and includes the purifying of the heart, Acts 15:8, 9.

"They are not of the world, even as I am not of the world." "Sanctify them through thy truth." John 17:1, 17.

Jesus evidently believed the disciples did not receive sanctification when they were converted and separated from the world, but that they should receive it as a second experience. He surely would not have prayed for something they already had. He believed it was a "divine act"— something his Father must do for them; He believed it was an experience to be realized in this life, for He was not praying for death.

SERMON OUTLINES.

PERFECT LOVE.

TEXT—*Herein is our love made perfect, that we may have boldness in the day of judgment:because as He is, so are we in this world. There is no fear in love; but perfect love casteth out fear: because fear hath torment. He that feareth is not made perfect in love.*— 1st John 4:17-18.

In almost every congregation there are three classes of people; first, those who are destitute of love and impelled by fear; second, those who have a measure of love mingled with fear; third, those who have love perfected and hence are without fear.

I. FEAR.

Slavish fear is the inevitable consequence of guilt. Sin makes men cowards. It is this alarm within that disturbs the rest of the sinner, and often through the mercy and grace of God, is appealed to by the Holy Spirit to bring men to repentance and salvation. Fear of penalty, fear of the judgment and fear of eternal damnation have led many to forsake sin and turn to God. The man who transgresses the law will naturally seek to evade and avoid the officers of the law. A guilty conscience needs no accuser. "The wicked flee when no man pursueth: but the righteous are bold as a lion." When Adam had sinned, he said, "I was afraid . . . and I hid myself."

II. LOVE.

The religion of Jesus Christ is *Love*. If a person have not love he may "speak with the tongues of men and of angels," "have the gift of prophesy and understand all mysteries, and all knowledge," and have "all faith," so that he could remove mountains, and bestow all his "goods to feed the poor" and even die a martyr by giving his "body to be burned" for what he believed to be the truth and yet it positively *profiteth him nothing*. "Love is the fulfilling of the law." This divine love in the heart is not something worked up, or the result of human effort, but "the love of God is shed abroad in our hearts by the Holy Ghost which is given unto us." "God is love; and he that dwelleth in love dwelleth in God, and God in him."

III. PERFECT LOVE.

All Christians have love, but all Christians have not perfect love. With many there is ever present the fear of man, the fear of ridicule or censure, and the fear of the judgment. While they love God, and are impelled by love to serve Him, they nevertheless have a continual inward conflict with fear, and at times have a real "torment" because of it. "Perfect love casteth out fear." "He that feareth is not made perfect in love." In justification love is imparted; in sanctification love is perfected. Perfect love is pure love in a pure heart, loving God perfectly with all the heart, soul, mind and strength and our neighbor as ourselves. It is called "perfect love," because that is the measure of love required.

We would note that "perfect love" is not obtained by growth or works, or any other human effort, but that the soul is *"made* perfect in love." It is a work divinely inwrought. A person cannot grow into regeneration because it is a work that God must do in him; exactly this is true concerning "perfect love." Again, we would note that "perfect love" is the proper fitness and preparation for the judgment. "Perfect love" and "holiness, without which no man shall see the Lord" are identical

AN UTTERMOST SALVATION

TEXT—*Wherefore He is able also to save them to the uttermost that come unto God by Him, seeing He ever liveth to make intercession for them.*—Heb. 7:25.

An uttermost salvation is the need of the race. In this chapter the apostle shows the superiority of the eternal, unchangeable priesthood of Christ as compared with that of Aaron's order, and urges that while "the law made nothing perfect, the bringing in of a better hope did." We will consider, first, *why He is able;* second, *the meaning or extent of an uttermost salvation,* and third, *to whom it is given.*

I. WHY HE IS ABLE.

It is important and comforting to note that the promise and possibility of a complete and uttermost salvation is conditioned on divine ability—*"He is able"*—and not on human resources or achievements. It is not a question as to what we can do, but what He can do. He is able, 1. Because in offering Himself as a sacrifice for sin, He was enabled to make a perfect and complete atonement for sin, and so to meet every demand of God and man. 2. He is able because He personally struggled with our common foe, and every power of evil we may encounter, and triumphed gloriously. His victory is the pledge of victory to His people and gives the assurance that we, too, may be "more than conquerors." 3. Because He has grace and power sufficient to sustain and keep His people in every trial of life—in all places and circumstances— and give victory over death. 4. Because He ever lives to perform within us all the purposes of His will and to plead for us in the presence of God. This seems to be the special argument of this chapter.

II. MEANING AND EXTENT OF UTTERMOST SALVATION.

1. *Meaning.* I quote from various commentaries and dictionaries. "To save in the most perfect manner, so that nothing shall be wanting to complete the salvation." "A power of working out complete deliverance for His people." "He is able always to save." "Always, and in and through all times, places and circumstances." "Altogether perfectly, so that nothing should be wanting afterwards, forever." "Utter," means "realized or developed to the last degree; entire and complete; beyond given limits; greatest possible extent; farthest point." According to this, it is to be saved altogether, always, perfectly, nothing wanting, beyond given limits, to the farthest point.

Extent. .It comprehends, the deliverance from, (a) the penalty of sin; "Jesus which delivered us from the wrath to come" (1 Thes. 1:10). (b) from the guilt of sin, "There is therefore now no condemnation to them which are in Christ Jesus" (Rom. 8:1). (c) From the pollution and defilement of sin. "He saved us by the washing of regeneration" (Tit. 3:5); "Ye are washed" (1 Cor. 6:11). (d) From the power of sin, "Sin shall not have dominion over you" (Rom. 6:14). (e) From the inbeing of sin, "The blood of Jesus Christ cleanseth us from all sin" (1 John 1:7); "But now being made free from sin and become servants to God, ye have your fruit unto holiness, and the end everlasting life" (Rom. 6:22). If Jesus Christ can save from any sin He can save from all sin. "Where sin abounded, grace did much more abound."

III. TO WHOM GIVEN.

All who "come unto God by Him." This implies a willingness to forsake all sin, to renounce all self-righteousness, and to yield a willing and unconditional obedience to Him. It means a personal approach to God in and by and through the merits of Jesus Christ. "I am the way, the truth and the life: no man cometh unto the Father but by Me." "Neither is there salvation in any other; for there is none other name under heaven given among men whereby we must be saved." "Whosoever transgresseth, and abideth not in the doctrine of Christ, hath not God." No man doubting and denying the divinity of Christ can know an uttermost salvation.

FULL SALVATION.

Text—*But of Him are ye in Christ Jesus, who of God is made unto us wisdom, and righteousness, and sanctification, and redemption.*—1 Cor. 1:30.

Full salvation comprehends the full provisions of the Gospel for soul, body and spirit. Through sin, the entire man has been wrecked, and Christ has come to fully restore to us all that we have lost by reason of sin. "Where sin abounded, grace did much more abound." To be full partakers of the benefits of the atonement of Christ, we must first be *"in* Christ." As the branch in united to the vine, so intimately must we be united to Jesus Christ This means more than faith in a historic Christ, or mere intellectual assent to truth; it means a personal contact and vital union, so as to partake of his life and nature. "If any man be in Christ, he is a new creature; old things are passed away;. behold all things are. become new." When this radical change takes place the individual will know about it. "Whosoever abideth in Him, sinneth not." If a man is not saved from sinning he is not saved at all. "If a man abideth not in Me, he is cast forth as a branch, and is withered and men gather them and cast them into the fire and they are burned." From these and similar passages, we see the importance of being *"in* Christ." When "in Christ" we will find that "His divine power hath given unto us all things that pertain unto life and godliness."

I. WISDOM.

One of the saddest features of sin is that it darkens the mind and shuts out the knowledge of God. The god of this world hath blinded the minds of them which believe not, lest the light of the glorious Gospel of Christ, who is the image of God, should shine unto them." The man in sin is blinded to his own best good and highest interest; neither does he realize his great peril. "The fear of the Lord is the beginning of wisdom." "Christ, in whom are hid all the treasures of wisdom and knowledge."—Col. 2:2, 3. "If any of you lack wisdom, let him ask of God, who giveth to all men liberally, and upbraideth not; and it shall be given him."

II. RIGHTEOUSNESS.

Adam Clark says of the word righteousness that it "means God's method of saving sinners." Through the transforming power of the Gospel, an unrighteous man is changed into a righteous man. "Abraham believed God, and it *was* counted unto him for righteousness." "As by one man's disobedience many were made sinners, so by the obedience of one shall many be made righteous." "To him that worketh not, but believeth on Him that justifieth the ungodly, his faith is counted for righteousness."

III. SANCTIFICATION.

"This is the will of God, even your sanctification." Sanctification is "the act of divine grace whereby we are made holy." While justification deals with sins committed, sanctification eradicates inbred sin. Sanctification is an experience for believers only, and is conditioned upon entire consecration and faith, subsequent to pardon. Justification delivers from guilt and condemnation; sanctification delivers from unholy tempers and sinful appetites.

"Christ also loved the Church and gave Himself for it, that He might sanctify and cleanse it." God, the Father, wills our sanctification. Christ, the Son, provided it, and the Holy Ghost accomplishes it.

IV. REDEMPTION.

Full redemption includes the body, and will be realized when this corruptible shall have put on incorruption, and this mortal shall have put on immortality. Blessed hope and promise of immortality. But, even now, "If the spirit of him that raised up Jesus from the dead dwell in you, He that raised up Christ from the dead shall also quicken your mortal bodies by His Spirit that dwelleth in you." So far as our spiritual nature is concerned, there is complete redemption now.

THE TWO BAPTISMS.

Text: *I indeed baptize you with water unto repentance but He that cometh after me is mightier than I, whose shoes I am not worthy to loose; He shall baptize you with the Holy Ghost, and with fire.—Matt. 3:11.*

In Jewish history, Pentecost was the festival which marked the conclusion of the harvest commenced with the Passover fifty days before, called "the feast of weeks." Among Christians it is the third of the chief festivals and designates the whole period from Easter to Pentecost, and is especially significant and celebrated because of the descent and outpouring of the Holy Spirit. It marked a new epoch and was the ushering in of a new dispensation. It was the fulfillment of prophecy, Peter declaring, "This is that which was spoken by the prophet Joel; and it shall come to pass in the last days, saith God, I will pour out of my spirit upon all flesh: and your sons and your daughters shall prophesy," etc. It was the fulfillment of the words of this text, as spoken by John the Baptist. Not only should we know of an historic Pentecost, but we should know of an individual, experimental Pentecost. The words of our text speak of two baptisms; one administered by John: the other administered by Christ.

JOHN'S BAPTISM.

John's baptism was an "indeed" baptism and was the outward seal and sign of an inward experience. John did not baptize just any one who applied. First, he preached and required genuine repentance, and demanded that they "bring forth fruits meet for repentance." (Matt. 3:7-9.) Genuine repentance includes the confession and forsaking of all sin. He who has not abandoned and forsaken all sin has not truly repented. Second, John preached that genuine repentance would bring the "remission of sins."—Luke 3:3. Third, when people had truly repented and received the remission of sins, there was to be a "knowledge of salvation." Not a "hope so," but a *know so* salvation; they were to know they had it. Fourth, he preached "that they should believe on him who should come after him, that is, on Christ Jesus."—Acts 19:4. Fifth, he preached that "He that believeth on the Son hath everlasting life."—John 3:26-36. So we see that John's converts had no superficial experience, but had genuine conversion. Yet it was distinctly declared and understood that John's ministry was simply to "Prepare the way of the Lord." It was simply preparing them for Christ's baptism, showing clearly that the baptism with the Holy Ghost is a *second* experience for truly justified people only.

CHRIST'S BAPTISM.

We need to distinguish between the *birth* of the Spirit and the *baptism* with the Spirit. These terms represent two distinct experiences. In the nature of things the birth must precede the baptism. Christ was the gift of God to the world; the Holy Ghost is the gift of God to the church—not to the world. Jesus said positively, while speaking of the Holy Ghost. "Whom the world cannot receive."—John 14:17. There are three words used in Scripture to denote the relation of the believer to the Holy Spirit, namely, the words, "upon," "with," and "in." To have the Holy Spirit "upon "us is to have special enduement of power for the highest efficiency and the accomplishment of the special callings in divine services.—Acts 1:8. To have the Holy Spirit "with" us is the relation of justified believers before they are wholly sanctified. Jesus said to his desciples, (who were truly justified), "He dwelleth with you," and gave them that deeper promise, "And shall be in you."—John 14:17. Thus we see that to have the Holy Spirit *in* us, is that measure which is granted to the sanctified believer to purify the heart. Peter, in explaining what transpired at the house of Cornelius, says, "God gave them the Holy Ghost even as He did unto us, purifying their hearts by faith." Hence we see that the baptism with the Holy Ghost includes the purifying of the heart by faith. Second, it is the impartation of power; power to abstain from all evil; power to perform and execute all the will of God; power to suffer patiently all the will of God permits us to suffer. Third, the baptism with the Holy Ghost means an infilling—"they were all filled." The valley of the Nile has been famous for its fertility for thousands of years. This fertility is due to the annual overflow of the Nile. We need the overflow to save this country from a spiritual famine.

HOLINESS OR HELL: WHICH?

TEXT:—*Follow peace with all men, and holiness, without which no man shall see the Lord.* .Heb. 12:14.

The subject, as stated above, may at first appear rather emphatic and startling, but in its last analysis is simply the plain teaching of the Bible, and of all evangelical denominations. All Christians believe that heaven is a holy place, and that no sin can enter there. Hence, if men are not made holy they cannot enter heaven, and if they cannot enter heaven they must take up their abode with the lost.

HOLINESS.

Commanded: As He which hath called you is holy, so be ye holy.—1 Peter 1:15, 16.

Called to holiness: God hath not called us unto uncleanness, but unto holiness.—1 Thess. 4:7.

Chosen to holiness: He hath chosen us in Him before the foundation of the world, that we should be holy and without blame before Him in love.—Eph. 1:4.

Chastised to bring us to holiness: Our fathers "Chastened us after their own pleasure, but He for our profit, that we might be partakers of His holiness." (Heb. 12:10.)

Holiness realized and perfected: "Having therefore these promises, dearly beloved, let us cleanse ourselves from all filthiness of the flesh and spirit, perfecting holiness in the fear of God."—2 Cor. 7:1.

Established in holiness: To the end He may establish your hearts unblameable in holiness before God, even our Father.—1 Thess. 3:13.

Holiness lived: That we being delivered out of the hand of our enemies might serve Him without fear, in holiness and righteousness before Him all the days of our life.—Luke 1:74, 75.

Holiness provided: Christ also loved the Church and gave Himself for it; that He might sanctify and cleanse it . . . that it should be holy and without blemish.—Eph. 5:25-27.

Holiness experienced: Holy men of God spake as they were moved by the Holy Ghost.—2 Pet. 1:21.

After this manner in the old time the holy women also, who trusted in God, adorned themselves.—2 Pet. 3:5.

What excuse can there be for men not to be holy?

THE DESTINY OF THOSE WHO REFUSE HOLINESS.

The Bible speaks of it as:

"Hell," (Matt. 5:29, 30; 10:28.)

"Hell fire," (Matt. 18:9; 5:22.)

"Furnace of fire," (Matt. 13:42, 50.)

"Unquenchable fire," (Luke 3:17; Mark 9:43-46.)

"Lake of fire," (Rev. 20:14, 15.)

"Fire and brimstone," (Rev. 21:8; 19:20.)
"Outer darkness," (Matt. 8:12; 22:13.)
"Everlasting destruction," (2 Thess. 1:9.)
"Everlasting punishment," (Matt. 25:46.)
"Eternal damnation," (Mark 3:29.)
"The bottomless pit," (Rev. 20:1.)

WHO THE INHABITANTS WILL BE.

"The Devil and his angles," (Mat. 25:41.)
'The wicked shall be turned into hell, and all the nations that forget God." (Psa. 9:17.)
"Them that know not God, and obey not the Gospel of our Lord Jesus Christ." (2 Thess. 1:8.)
"All things that offend, and *them which do iniquity.*" (Matt. 13:41.)
"The fearful, and unbelieving, and the abominable, and murderers, and whoremongers, and sorcerers, and idolaters, and all liars, shall have their part in the lake which burneth with fire and brimstone." (Rev. 21:8.)
"And whosoever was not found written in the book of life was cast into the lake of fire," (Rev. 20:15.)

Hell is a necessity not only as a punishment for the lawless, but as a protection for the law abiding.

Hell was not created for men and was never intended for them, but was *"prepared* for the Devil and his angels." He who goes there goes as an intruder.

God does not send men to hell; they go there as the result of their own choice. Men can be saved if they will be.

Hell is dreadful because of the correspondence between

the characters who go there and the place; also because of what is not there. There is no law, no love, no hope, no truth and no rest in hell. Even the lost in hell pray against others coming there. (Luke 16:28.)

HOLINESS VERSUS BACKSLIDING.

TEXT—*If after they have escaped the pollutions of the world through the knowledge of the Lord and Saviour Jesus Christ, they are again entangled therein, and overcome, the latter end is worse with them than the beginning. For it had been better for them not to have known the way of righteousness, than, after they have known it, to turn from the holy commandment delivered unto them.—II Pet. 2:20-21.*

Immobility is inconsistent with our being, mentally, physically or spiritually. We either advance or retrograde; increase or decrease; especially is this true of our spiritual life; there is no standing still. The sin of omission terminates in sins of commission. The way to keep from backsliding is to persistently and obediently press forward. To rest in a past experience is perilous and soon leaves the soul destitute of saving grace. "For we are made partakers of Christ, if we hold the beginning of our confidence steadfast unto the end." Some lessons from the text are: (1) There is an escape from the pollutions of the world. (2) The way of escape. (3) That holiness is imperative. (4) That holiness is a second experience. (5) The latter end of a backslider worse than the beginning.

I. AN ESCAPE.

There is a way out of sin and the pollutions of the world. Thank God! Sin pollutes, corrupts and degrades everything contaminated thereby. Oh, the filthiness of sin! A sin polluted heart means polluted thoughts, polluted words, polluted life. Hence David said, "He brought me up also out of an horrible pit, out of the miry clay."

II. THE WAY OF ESCAPE.

"Escaped * * * through the knowledge of the Lord and Savior Jesus Christ." An experimental knowledge of salvation can only come to the soul that has forsaken all sin and believed on the Lord Jesus Christ. He is "the way, the truth, and the life." His name is called "Jesus; for He shall save His people from their sins;" "who gave Himself for our sins, that He might deliver us from this present evil world, according to the will of God." "Neither is there salvation in any other; for there is none other name under heaven given among men, whereby we must be saved."

III. HOLINESS IMPERATIVE.

Holiness is the Bible standard. Holiness is freedom from sin. There is nothing mysterious about this subject. If a man is done with sin he wants holiness; when a man does not want holiness it is evident he wants sin; there is nothing else to want. God commands, "Be ye holy." It is not optional but imperative. To disobey is sin. No person can disobey His word and retain His favor. "Follow peace with all men and holiness, without which no man shall see the Lord."

IV. A SECOND EXPERIENCE.

It was those who "have escaped the pollution of the world," and "have known the way of righteousness," "after they have known it," "turn from the holy commandment." What is "the holy commandment?" Undoubtedly the commandment to be holy. Thus we see that the commandment to be holy is to those who have already "escaped" and know "the way of righteousness." Hence we see that backsliding is the result of "turning from" the commandment to be holy.

V. WORSE THAN BEGINNING.

This is so because increased light brings increased responsibility, and increased condemnation. It is "worse" because it destroys confidence in one's self and in religion in general. Such an one is apt to say, "I have tried it once, and can't hold out." It is "worse" because of the destructive influence it has on others and thus augments guilt. It is "worse" because of the torment and tortures memory will inflict in hell, when it shall be said, "Son, remember."

HEAVENLY MINDEDNESS.

TEXT—*Let this mind be in you, which was also in Christ Jesus: who, being in the form of God, thought it not robbery to be equal with God: but made Himself of no reputation, and took upon Him the form of a servant, and was made in the likeness of men.—Phil 2:5-7.*

Not only is it ours to believe on Christ, but to be indwelt by the very mind of Christ. Whoever is willing to have his own carnal mind destroyed may "have the mind of Christ."

The text urges the mind of Christ with particular reference to His humiliation. In order to have a proper appreciation of His condescending love, we need to apprehend some of His glory before His humiliation.

I. WHO AND WHERE HE WAS.

He was one with the Father. John 10:30, 38. He "was with God:" Yea He "was God." John 1:1. "All things were created by Him, and for Him: and He is before all things, and by Him all things consist." Col. 1:16, 17. "God * * * hath in these last days spoken unto us by His Son, whom He hath appointed heir of all things, by whom also He made the worlds; who being the brightness of His glory, and the express image of His person, and upholding all things by the word of His power." Heb. 1:2, 3. He could say, "He that hath seen Me hath seen the Father."

He was in the bosom of the Father, "heir of all things," attended by angels, "upholding all things by the word of His power" encircled with light and glory unto which no being could approach, but emptied Himself, laying aside the *effulgence* of His *glory,* became a servant, and humbled Himself even unto the death of the cross.

II. HIS HUMILIATION.

"He, who was the Son of God, became the Son of man, that we who were the sons of men might become the sons of God." The babe of Bethlehem, the man of Galilee, the Lamb of Calvary—how marvelous and overwhelming the contrast. "Of no reputation," despised and rejected of men; a wanderer, with no place to lay His head; washing the disciples' feet—the servant of all; buffeted, spit upon, in the hands of a mob—crucified. "He was oppressed, and He was afflicted, yet He opened not His mouth; He is brought as a lamb to the slaughter, and as a sheep before her shearers is dumb, so He opened not His mouth. He was taken from prison and from judgment: and who shall declare His generation? for He was cut off out of the land of the living and He made His grave with the wicked, and with the rich in His death: because He had done no violence, neither was any deceit in His mouth." What a picture of the *omnipotent, eternal, infinite God!* And all this to save a poor sinner.

III. "LET THIS MIND BE IN YOU."

"The heart is deceitful above all things, and desperately wicked: who can know it?" Out of the heart are the issues of life. Resolutions, and will power can never change a heart that boasts and glories in its very shame. While the self-life remains, a man will become "vainly puffed up by his fleshly mind." Before we can manifest His outward lowliness and meekness and humility the "carnal mind" which "is enmity against God" must be utterly destroyed. It is death to all self-will, self-seeking, selfish ambitions and self-exaltation. Instead of being in the service of God for what we may be able to get out of it, we shall then be in the service of God for what we may put into it; to serve rather than to be served. A holy heart, made so by the blood of Jesus Christ, and the transforming power of the gospel, alone can bring the individual where "this mind is in you." "He that saith He abideth in Him, ought himself also so to walk, *even as He walked.*"

CHRIST THE WAY.

TEXT: *Jesus said unto him, I am the way, the truth and the life; no man cometh unto the Father, but by me.* John 14:6.

This text is generally divided into three parts, each part independent of the other parts. But this is not so. The text is a unity. Christ had told His disciples that He was going to prepare a place for them in His Father's house, adding, "and whither I go ye know, and the way ye know." Thomas replied, "Lord, we know not whither thou goest; and how can we know the way?" The question of Thomas involved an inquiry with reference to a single thing—"the way:" so Christ's reply was an answer involving only a single thing. The words *truth* and *life* were only used as they had reference to the great fact announced. "I am the way,"—the word truth expressing the character of 'the way;" the word life as expressing the direction and end of "the way;" as if Christ had said, "I am the truthful way which leads to life."

Christ did not say, "I am a way," but, "I am *the* way;" He only is "the way" to God; "no man cometh unto the Father, but by me." This declaration means death to Unitarianism and Swedenborgianism, and every other cult and pretense that ignores or denies the divinity of Christ.

FROM WHAT AND TO WHAT THE WAY LEADS.

From death to life: Spiritual life is three-fold in its character, having a principle, an essence, and a development. The principle of spiritual life is faith in God; the essence of spiritual life is love to God; and the development of spritual life is obedience to God; this three-fold aspect of spiritual life corresponds exactly with man's three-fold capacity of moral character, expressed by the words intellect, sensibilities and conduct. A man may think right, feel right and act right. "He that believeth on the Son hath everlasting life." Faith is lodged in the intellect. "We know that we have passed from death unto life, because we love.' "He that loveth not knoweth not God." Love is lodged in the sensibilities. "He that hath my commandments, and keepeth them, he it is that loveth me . . and I will love him, and will manifest myself to him." Development of spiritual life is conditioned on obedience which is lodged in conduct. 'And you hath He quickened who were dead in trespasses and sins."

From darkness to light. Sin plunges the soul into darkness, so that a man dying without Christ, always crosses the river of death in midnight darkness. "In Him was life; and the life was the light of men." "I am the light of the world: He that followeth me shall not walk in darkness, but shall have the light of life." "God, who commanded the light to shine out of darkness, hath shined in our hearts, to give the light of the knowledge of the glory of God in the face of Jesus Christ." "God is light, and in Him is no darkness at all. If we say that we have fellowship with Him, and walk in darkness, we lie, and do not the truth."

From sin to holiness. "Ye know that He was manifested to take away our sins." "If we walk in the light, as He is in the light, we have fellowship one with another, and the blood of Jesus Christ His Son cleanseth us from all sin." "Now being made free from sin, and become servants to God, ye have your fruit unto holiness, and the end everlasting life."

He is the way from bondage to liberty; from weakness to strength, from sadness to gladness; from earth to heaven He is the only way, a living way, an accessable way, a plain way, a perpetual way and a sure way.

"Neither is there salvation in any other; for there is none other name under heaven given among men, whereby we must be saved."

SECRETS OF VICTORY.

Text: In all these things we are more than conquerors through Him that loved us. Rom. 8:37.

The Church of Jesus Christ is frequently likened to an army, and we are exhorted to "endure hardness, as a good soldier of Jesus Christ," and "fight the good fight of faith." There can be no victory without conflict and battle. The greater the battle, the grander the victory. To be a conqueror in all the conflicts of life means much; but to be *"more* than conquerors," means more. It means that the victories are gained with some rounds of ammunition left, as in the case of David and Goliath; he slew Goliath with his first round of ammunition and came back with four rounds of ammunition left, ready for four more giants. To be "more than conquerors," means that you take some spoils, as in the case of Jehosaphat and his army against the children of Ammon, Moab, and the people of Mount Sier, where the victory was so glorious it took them three days to gather up the spoils. 2 Chron. 20:25. To be "more than conqueror" means that you are continually taking advanced ground; that the ashes of your camp-fires will not be found two nights in the same place. Such a life is the privilege of all saints. Note some secrets of this victorious life.

1. CONVICTION.

Mere intellectual assent to truth does not make men soldiers. The fellow who believes just as the last man he met, and is on both sides of the question—is what is known as a policy man—is no good. He is what Dr.

Bresee would call a "putty fellow." Like the man, when asked what he believed, said, he "believed just as the church believed." When asked what the church believed, said, "the church believes as I believe;" when asked what he and the church together believed, he was quite sure they both together believed exactly the same thing—but did not know what it was. A good soldier has deep rooted convictions—really believes some things—and believes them with all his heart. Convictions divinely inwrought by the Holy Ghost that Jesus Christ can save from all sin—within and without—is the contention of our church. *Salvation from all sin,* is our battle cry. Sentimental folk are not the kind that heroes, and warriors, and martyrs are made of.

II. VICTORY WITHIN.

The "old man" is an enemy of God and an ally of Satan. While he is within he will betray you into the hands of the enemy. An inward foe is more to be feared than outward foes. The destruction of inbred sin brings inward rest and victory. A civil war means the division of forces and leaves the nation a prey to other powers. One of the advantages of the sanctified life is that "we wrestle not against flesh and blood, but against principalities, against powers," etc., all of which are without. Hence David prayed, "Unite my heart to fear thy name." Ps. 86:11. Inward victory is the secret of outward victory. If you would have victory on the field of battle, you must first have perfect victory at home, which can only come by being sanctified wholly, and so have the carnal mind destroyed.

III. ENTIRE CONSECRATION.

Half heartedness means certain defeat. A devotion that will gladly yield up all, even life itself, is one of the essential secrets of victory. True consecration never stops to count the cost, when once the will of God is made clear. Such men will take joyfully the spoiling of their goods, and rejoice they are counted worthy to suffer persecution for His sake.

IV. FULL EQUIPMENT.

We are urged to "put on the whole armor of God, that ye may be able to stand." The first inference is that without the whole armor we may not be able to stand, and the second inference is that with the "whole armor" we will be able to stand. This armor will make one invulnerable, and more than a match for Satan. For description of same, read Eph. 6:11-16. In this armor there is no provision for the back, as we are expected to keep our face toward the foe. Many are wounded in the back because of compromise.

V. KNOWLEDGE OF RESOURCES.

To know that God and all the angels and all the resources of heaven are pledged to our victory will inspire great confidence. One man with God is always a majority. "The people that do know their God shall be strong and do exploits." "Victory is of the Lord." (Marg. Prov. 21:31). We ever need to remember that "the battle is not ours, but God's" He will make a highway through the sea, command the sun to stand still, cause the stars to fight against our enemies, stop the mouths of lions.

quench the fires that may be kindled, and turn the victory on Israel's side, if we will but trust Him. "Faith is the victory." Courage is faith on the battlefield. "They overcame him by the blood of the Lamb, and by the word of their testimony; and they loved not their lives unto the death." "Thanks be to God, which giveth us the victory through our Lord Jesus Christ."

SELF EXAMINATION.

TEXT. *Examine yourselves, whether ye be in the faith; prove your own selves... Know ye not your own selves, how that Jesus Christ is in you, except ye be reprobates?* —*2Cor.* 13:5.

Self examination may not be a pleasant task, but is certainly most essential and profitable. The text does not say that we should examine other people, but "*examine yourselves.*" The questions of our relations to God and eternal destiny are of such solemn import that we can not afford to be mistaken or deceived.

UNION WITH CHRIST.

The union of the believer with his Lord is a *reciprocal* union. "Abide in me, and I in you." This means more than assent to truth, or faith in a historic Christ, or subscribing your name to a creed; it means a personal contact and a vital union with Christ, as the vine and its branches, as the body and its members, as the head and the body. Then, as Luther has said, "All that Christ has, now becomes the property of the believing soul; all that the soul has, becomes the property of Christ. Christ possesses every blessing and eternal salvation; they are henceforth the property of the soul."

SOME EVIDENCES OF THIS UNION.

1. *Saved from sinning.* "Whosoever abideth in Him sinneth not; whosoever sinneth hath not seen Him, neither known Him."—1 John 3:6. Whosoever is not saved from sinning is not saved at all. A sinning religion is the devil's religion. "He that committeth sin is of the devil."—1 John 3:8.

2. *No condemnation.* "There is therefore now no condemnation to them which are in Christ Jesus."—Rom. 8:1. Sin and condemnation are inseparable. Whosoever commits sin is necessarily under condemnation, even though the soul does not realize its guilt all the while. "He that believeth not is condemned already."—John 3:18.

3. *A new creature.* "If any man be in Christ he is a new creature: old things are passed away; behold, all things are become new."—2 Cor. 5:17. To be in Christ means more than turning over a new leaf, the passing of a new resolution, or mere reformation; it is a new creation; a regeneration and transformation inwrought by the Holy Ghost.

4. *Spiritual life.* "He that hath the Son hath life."—1 John 5:12. There is no such thing as a dead Christian. "And you hath he quickened, who were dead in trespasses and sins." In Christ the soul will know the throbbings and pulsations of divine life. Jesus said, "I

am come that they might have life, and that they might have it more abundantly."—John 10:10.

5. *Fruitful.* "He that abideth in me, and I in him, the same bringeth forth much fruit."—John 15:5. Fruit is the spontaneous result of life. As Gordon has said, "The method of grace is precisely the reverse of the method of legalism. The latter is holiness in order to union with God, the former, union with God in order to holiness." We need to distinguish between works and fruit. "The fruit of the Spirit is love, joy, peace, longsuffering, gentleness, goodness, faith, meekness, temperance; against such there is no law."—Gal. 5:22,23.

THE EXAMINATION.

"Christ in you" excludes all that is not Christly. The soul may be compared to a seven story building, as follows: The will; the affections; the thoughts; the appetites; the tempers; the motives; and the secret life. The investigation and examination should go through all these various departments and see that *the Christ attitude* dominates and fills each department. Only the light of the Holy Spirit, by the Word of God can disclose to us our real inwardness. "Behold, thou desirest truth in the inward parts; and in the hidden part thou shalt make me to know wisdom."

A reprobate is one abandoned as hopelessly wicked, or to a hopeless doom.

GLORYING IN THE CROSS.

Text—*But God forbid that I should glory save in the cross of our Lord Jesus Christ, by whom the world is crucified unto me, and I unto the world.*—Gal. 6:14.

> "In the cross of Christ I glory,
> Towering o'er the wrecks of time,
> All the light of sacred story,
> Gathers 'round its head sublime."

The cross is mentioned in three different senses in the Bible. It is important to distinguish them. First, it is used to signify *the wooden cross,* upon which the Lord Jesus was crucified. Second, it is used to signify *the way of salvation* by Jesus Christ crucified. Third, it is used to signify the *sufferings that come to us in following Christ.*

I. THE WOODEN CROSS.

As an instrument of death, the cross was of Roman invention and was used only in case of slaves, or very notorious criminals, and malefactors of the basest sort. This was the death to which Jesus stooped. "He endured the cross, despising the shame." In the cross we see the stern, unrelenting hand of justice exacting the penalty of the law for sin, and also the unfathomable love of God for a lost world. The cross speaks to us of substitution, of reconciliation, of peace with God, and of life eternal.

II. THE CROSS, THE WAY OF SALVATION.

This is the sense in which the word is used in the text. It is the name given to the whole plan of salvation by a crucified Redeemer. As in 1 Cor.1:18: "The preaching of the Cross is to them that perish foolishness, but unto us who are saved, it is the power of God." Glorying in the Cross means the renunciation of all self righteousness, and of all the law and an entire reliance upon and acceptance of the finished work of Calvary as the only hope for a sinner. Glorying in the Cross means not only that we endure the Cross but that we delight in it, and go with Him to the Cross until we can say, "I am crucified with Christ" and so are "made conformable unto His death." Crucifixion is the divine method for the self-life,—the carnal mind which we inherited. "Knowing this, that our old man is crucified with Him." Rom. 6:6. This is the "second blessing, properly so called." In justification our spiritual sensibilities are quickened and made alive; in sanctification our carnal sensibilities are crucified and deadened.

III. THE CROSS TO BE BORNE.

"If any man will come after me, let him deny himself, and take up his cross and follow me." In following Christ a man may meet with scorn and ridicule and persecution and adversity. All that will live godly in Christ Jesus shall suffer persecution. Obeying God should not be a question of expediency or of personal pleasure but a fixed and settled purpose of the heart, though it means suffering, and the loss of all things. A true Christian will do his or her duty even if they don't feel like it. "He that taketh not up the cross and followeth after Me, is not worthy of Me." No cross, no crown.

SEEKING THE FACE OF GOD.

TEXT:—*When thou saidst, seek ye my face; my heart said unto thee, Thy face, Lord, will I seek.—Psa. 27:8.*

The guilty may seek His favor; the obedient child of God will seek His face. We should seek Him, not simply for the loaves and fishes—something He has—but for *what He is.* There is a possibility of becoming more absorbed with an *"it"* than with *Him* who has made *"it"* possible.

Many are occupied with ceremonies and doctrines, which may be beautiful and helpful in their proper relations, but without the presence of the living Christ are simply dead and wearisome formalities; the shell without a kernel. Dean Stanley has well said: "The teachings of Christ are not *abstract* doctrines nor ceremonial regulations."

We need to come face to face with God; first, that we know Him, and, second, that we may know ourselves. Not until Isaiah could say: "Mine eyes have seen the King, the Lord of Hosts," did he understand his own heart and realize his moral uncleanness. "Where there is no vision the people perish." (Prov. xxix, 18.

The countenance is a reflecting mirror, wherein the thoughts and affections, otherwise invisible, appear. It is thereby that our inward emotions are made known to others: love, hatred, desire, dislike, joy, grief, confidence, despair, courage, cowardice, ambition, contempt, pride, modesty, cruelty, compassion and the rest of the affections are all reflected in the countenance.

To seek His face means:

1. *Walking in light.* "They shall walk, O Lord, in the light of Thy countenance." (Ps. lxxxix, 15.) The light of His countenance upon us implies His peculiar favor and blessing. "The face of the Lord is against them that do evil."

2. *Light in His light.* "In Thy light shall we see light." (Ps. xxxvi, 9.) To have the mind of Christ and see as He sees, we must seek His face. "Wherefore be ye not unwise, but understanding what the will of the Lord is." (Eph. v, 17.)

3. *Changed into His image.* "We all, with open face, beholding as in a glass the glory of the Lord, *are changed into the same image* from glory to glory, even as by the spirit of the Lord." (II Cor., iii, 18.) That is holiness. The spirit of the Lord changing us into the same image, while we behold "the glory of God in the face of Jesus Christ." "For whom He did foreknow, He also did predestinate to be conformed to the image of His Son, that He might be the first born among many brethren." (Rom. viii, 29.)

4. *Fellowship and communion.* "And the Lord spake unto Moses face to face, as a man speaketh unto his friend." (Ex. xxxiii, 11.) "If we say that we have fellowship with Him, and walk in darkness, we lie and do not the truth." "And truly our fellowship is with the Father and with His Son, Jesus Christ." (I John, i, 3.)

5. *Cause our face to shine.* "Moses wist not that the skin of his face shone while he talked with Him." (Ex. xxxiv, 29.) The scowls and frowns and dark looks all

disappear when we seek the face of God. Beulah dwellers have the lines of their countenances drawn from east to west, instead of north to south. "A merry heart maketh a cheerful countenance." "The help of *His* countenance" becomes "the *health* of my countenance." (Ps. xlii, 5, 11.)

6. *Fullness of joy.* "Thou shalt make me full of joy with thy countenance." (Acts, ii, 28.) "David speaketh concerning Him, I foresaw the Lord always before my face * * * therefore did my heart rejoice and my tongue was glad."

> "As by the light of opening day
> The stars are all concealed;
> So earthly pleasures fade away
> When Jesus is revealed."

ONE THING.

One thing thou lackest. Mark 10:21.
One thing is needful. Luke 10:42.
One thing have I desired of the Lord, that will I seek after. Ps. 27:4.
One thing I know. John 9:25.

Michael Angelo had never been so great a painter if his love of art had not become so enthusiastic that he frequently did not take off his garments to sleep for a whole week. It was his devotion to "one thing" that made him world-famed. It has been said that Mr. Moody had as his motto: "Consecrate and then concentrate," which meant the recognition of the same principle. Said Mr. Spurgeon, the great London preacher: "A man must have one pursuit, and consecrate all his powers to one effort, if he would excel or rise to eminence among his fellows."

1. "ONE THING THOU LACKEST."

These words were spoken by our Lord to a young man who made his boast that he kept all the law, and applies to every man in his unrenewed state. This young ruler was a moral man, and so far as we know his character was unimpeachable, but he nevertheless lacked saving faith in Jesus Christ. Self-righteousness will not avail, for we read, "All our righteousnesses are as filthy rags." Men may boast of morality, good works, and many commendable traits and qualities, but without Christ as a personal Savior enthroned within, the essential thing is ever lacking, and the soul lost. "Examine yourselves whether ye be in the faith; prove your own selves. Know ye not your own selves, how that Jesus Christ is in you, except ye be reprobates." 2 Cor., 13:5.

2. ONE THING IS NEEDFUL.

These words were spoken to Martha, a true-hearted disciple. She had received Jesus, and was serving him by providing for His entertainment. Still there was "one thing needful." She has not sufficient grace to keep her from being "cumbered," "careful" and "troubled about many things." In other words, she was not saved from stewing, fretting and worrying when things were not altogether to her liking. How many Christians today may be said to be *Martha-fied* in that they have this inward unrest. In saying to Mary she had "chosen that good part," he was not speaking of good in opposition to bad; but of two good ways of pleasing and serving the Lord, Mary had chosen the better. Both were true-hearted disciples, but the one was absorbed in the higher, the other in the lower of two ways of honoring their Lord, Jesus has a deeper interest in our own relation and attitude toward Him than in our "much serving." While the world and a formal church places great premium on *doing*, Jesus emphasizes the *being* as of first importance. Martha needed the "second blessing" to deliver her from carnality, the root of all undue anxiety, and fretting and impatience. "Much serving" so engrossed her she missed her Lord's teaching. To become absorbed with work—though it be religious work—so as not to find time to wait at His feet, is to fail of "that good part which shall not be taken away."

3. ONE THING TO SEEK AFTER.

The lesson I would impress from these words is the importance of definite seeking. Praying in a half-hearted, indefinite way will never bring any blessing. A sinner might pray for pardon in an indefinite manner for forty years, but would never receive pardon. Finally he becomes desperate and definitely sets about settling this "one thing," and soon obtains pardon. Exactly the same is true of a believer seeking sanctification. It requires earnest seeking and definite seeking of the "one thing" to find either pardon or cleansing. You cannot seek God and at the same time seek the emoluments of men.

4. "ONE THING I KNOW."

This was the testimony of the blind man to whom Jesus had restored his sight. He might not be able to explain the science or philosophy of his experience, but he positively knew "one thing," that whereas he had been blind he could now see. So we may know when our sins are pardoned, because "the Spirit itself beareth witness with our spirit, that we are the children of God." And in like manner we know when we are sanctified. "For by one offering he hath perfected for ever them that are sanctified; whereof the Holy Ghost also is a witness to us." (Heb. 10:14, 15.) Thank God for a "know-so" salvation.

LEPROSY A TYPE OF SIN.

TEXT:—*"And, behold, there came a leper and worshipped Him, saying, Lord, if thou wilt, thou canst make me clean. And Jesus put forth his hand, and touched him, saying, I will; be thou clean. And immediately his leprosy was cleansed. Matt. 8:2-3.*

Leprosy is one of the Bible's representatives of the intense malignity and defilement of the mortal malady that has attacked you and me, namely, *Sin.*

Leprosy and sin are analogous, viz,:
1. All classes alike subject to it.
2. Is of small beginning.
3. Loathsome—repulsive.
4. Incurable by human skill and human agencies.
5. Contagious—diffusive.

6. Results in separation and banishment.

7. Terminates in death.

Leprosy is especially a type of inbred sin because:

1. It is transmitted to posterity—hereditary.

2. It is a constitutional disease—a condition, not an act.

3. It was never pardoned—but cleansed away.

a. This man, by his very earnest petition, recognized and acknowledged his condition. That is the first step toward the kingdom. "He that covereth his sins shall not prosper: but whoso confesseth and forsaketh them shall have mercy." "If we confess our sins He is faithful and just to forgive them."

b. He had unquestioning and unwavering faith in the power and ability of Jesus to heal him, saying, "Thou canst." "Without faith it is impossible to please Him: for he that cometh to God must believe that He is, and that He is a rewarder of them that diligently seek Him." Salvation must be by faith alone, that it may be by grace alone.

c. He manifested proper humility. Luke says he "fell on his face," (Luke 5:12.) "God resisteth the proud, but giveth grace unto the humble." The way up is down. He "stooped to conquer, and he conquered by stooping." By giving in to God we win.

d. "Immediately his leprosy was cleansed." The cure was instantaneous. So it is in pardon. With one word— one touch— all the guilt is swept away. In like manner the deliverance from inbred sin is instantaneous. A *gradatim* destruction of the "old man" is as unreasonable as it is unscriptural. There is a gradual approach to the blessing so far as the human side of sanctification is concerned, but when the consecration is entire and faith perfect, the work of cleansing is instantaneously, divinely inwrought.

"The Blood cleanseth" is always in the present tense.

BEYOND THE SECOND VEIL.

Text: Heb. 10:19-22.

The service and worship of God as instituted and indicated by the ceremonial law and Levitical priesthood consisted in types and shadows "of good things to come," says the Apostle (Heb. 10:1.) The text at once introduces us to some of these "good things."

Whereas the sacrifices under the law failed in making the comers thereto perfect, and the entrance into the holiest was only possible by dead sacrifices, Christ by His sacrificial offering has consecrated and opened up a new and living way—"Because the living and life-giving Savior is that way." While the blood of bulls and of goats could not take away sin, the blood of Jesus can—hence we come in confidence and "full assurance of faith," having our hearts sprinkled from an evil conscience and so have. boldness or liberty to enter into the holiest.

The steps for entering the holiest by the high priest doubtless have their spiritual significance, and will indicate to us the manner of approach and entrance upon the experience signified by "the holiest."

The Tabernacle was the sacred tent where man met God

in close communion, and was built after a model given to Moses by Jehovah. It was used in the exodus, on the journey to Canaan, and in the Promised Land until Solomon built the temple on Zion, after which it is mentioned no more. Every Bible reader knows that this Tabernacle was divided into two rooms called the holy place and most holy place, or the "holy of holies."

The first is typical of the regenerated life, as here was found the candle-stick and shew-bread which signifies light and life; but if the oil was not daily replenished the lights would go out, and the bread became stale if not constantly renewed. Then there was the veil between the worshipper and his God.

Before entering the holiest the high priest must:

1. Be washed with water. Lev. 8:6; Ex. 29:4. This signifies a clean outward life.

2. He must put on "holy garments" called "garments to consecrate him," Ex. 28:3-4. This was made of pure white linen. No mixture of wool was allowed, Ezek. 44:17-18. Wool would cause "sweat" and "sweat" is the badge of bondage. How many whose linen is mixed with the "wool" of carnality, causing "sweat" in the discharge of what they call "doing their duty." Entire consecration puts an end to "sweat," as duty becomes a delight, and obedience a luxury. The veil was rent when Jesus died, Matt. 27:51.

3. The application of blood on the right ear, thumb and great toe, Ex. 29:20; Lev. 8:23. Speaking of this application of the blood, Paul says, "purged with blood," Heb. 9:22. Consecration is not sanctification. Consecration is the human side while the cleansing by the Blood

is the Divine side of sanctification. "The blood of Jesus Christ His Son cleanseth us from all sin," 1 Jno. 1:7.

4. Subsequent to the blood applied was the anointing oil, Ex. 29:7-21; Lev. 8:12. The oil signifies the anointing of the Holy Spirit. The heart being cleansed the Comforter takes up His abode, in His pentecostal fullness and power.

In the Holiest of all there is:

1. The golden censer—prayer and praise.
2. The Divine presence as signified by "the Ark of the Covenant."
3. Hidden manna—preserved, heavenly diet—imported supplies.
4. Fruitfulness—as signified by Aaron's rod; before being placed there it was just a dry stick.
5. The ineffable glory—shadowing the mercy seat.

In the holiest of all there was: safety—divine protection; communion, Ex. 25:22; quietness—a hidden life —rest—satisfaction—blessing for others, Lev. 9:22:23 —fullness of joy, Lev. 9:24—The badge of holiness on forehead, Ex. 28:26-38—bell and pomegranate, Ex. 28: 34-35.

The bell signifying profession.

Pomegranate signifying fruit—life.

ESSENTIAL TRUTH.

TEXT:—*"Continue in faith and charity and holiness."*

ALL TRUTH is essential in a relative sense, but all truth is not directly essential to salvation. Some lines of truth, must be recognized as the *conditions* of salvation, while other lines of truth have rather to do with the *results* of salvation. The text suggests three fundamental truths which are imperative and directly essential to salvation, neither of which can be omitted and the soul be saved. They are faith, charity and holiness. This text implies the possibility of having faith, charity and holiness in life; more, it implies that some one has come into possession of these graces; otherwise they could not be admonished or exhorted to *continue* in the same.

I. FAITH.

Faith is imperative. "Without faith it is impossible to please Him." (Heb. 11:6.) "He that believeth not shall be damned." Mark 16:16.

Faith means the renunciation of self, and dependence upon Christ alone as the source of righteousness and the hope of acceptance with God.

> Forsaking
> All
> I
> Take
> Him.

Faith is simply believing what God has said, and believing it *because* God said it, and thus appropriate His Word to our own hearts. It has greatly helped me to remember that His Word is a creative Word. When God said, "Let there be light," "there was light." His Word made it so. Faith must rest on the Word of God.

II. CHARITY.

Charity is divine love—the very essence of religion. "Though I bestow all my goods to feed the poor, and though I give my body to be burned, and have not charity, it profiteth me nothing." A person might die a martyr in his devotion and conviction to what he regarded religion, if he "have not charity, it profiteth him nothing." We hear it said, it does not matter so much what is believed if the individual is but sincere: but the Scriptures teach that a man may believe a lie and be damned, (2 Thes. 2:10-11.) In believing the truth, "the love of God is shed abroad in our hearts by the Holy Ghost." "He that loveth not, knoweth not God; for God is love. He that dwelleth in love dwelleth in God, and God in him." In the Greek language there are two words for love: the word *Philia,* signifying human love; the word *Agape,* signifying divine love. Charity refers to the latter. *Philia,* or human love, is fickle and subject to circumstances. *Agape,* or divine love, will pray for an enemy, and with a rugged tree as a dying couch, will say, "Father, forgive them."

III. HOLINESS.

This, too, is imperative, for we read, "follow peace with all men, and holiness, without which no man shall see the Lord." Holiness is the condition and fitness for seeing God. God is holy, and heaven is holy, and the angels are holy, hence we must be holy if we would enter there. Holiness is freedom from sin. God has commanded us to be holy, called us to be holy, chosen us to be holy, chastised us that we should be holy and made the provision ample for us to be holy, hence we are left without excuse for not being holy. "If we walk in the light . . . the blood of Jesus Christ His Son cleanseth us from all sin." Holiness is pure love in a pure heart. No man can make an honest pretense to love God, who is the essence and embodiment of holiness, and be averse or antagonistic to holiness.

Faith is the passport to love, love is the passport to holiness, and holiness is the passport to heaven. Neither can be neglected without peril to the soul.

JESUS CHRIST—THE GOD-MAN.

TEXT—*What think ye of Christ? Whose son is He?*—Matt. 22:42.

If we do not think right toward him we will not know how to act right toward Him. As some one has said, "Sow a thought, and reap a desire; sow desire and reap an act; sow an act and reap a habit; sow a habit and reap a character; sow a character and reap destiny." Thought was the foundation of character and destiny. "For as he thinketh in his heart, so is he." Prov. 23:7. "The Lord knoweth the thoughts of man." "The thoughts of the wicked are an abomination to the Lord." Prov. 15:26. Hence, He requires that "the wicked forsake his way, and the unrighteous man his thoughts." There is a maxim that says, "You cannot hang a man for his thoughts." That, perhaps, is true; but we need, nevertheless, to remember that a man may be damned for his thoughts. "For the Lord searcheth all hearts, and understandeth all the imaginations of the thoughts." I Chron. 28:9. Conduct is but the fruit of your thoughts. It is evident that no man thinks right of Christ who does not receive Him as a personal Savior and gladly obey Him.

It may help us to right thinking and right conclusions to know what they thought of Him who had personally known Him. So we will ask both His friends and his enemies to bear witness to Him.

HIS ENEMIES.

Pilate: He heard the charges against Him and himself examined Him, and then said: "I find no fault in this man." Luke, 23:4.

Pilate's Wife: She sent a message to her husband, while Christ was on trial, saying: "Have thou nothing to do with that just man." Matt. 27:19. She believed Him to be a *just* man.

Judas Iscariot: After having associated with Jesus three years he betrayed Him for "thirty pieces of silver." But hear his testimony: "I have sinned in that I have betrayed the innocent blood." Matt. 27:4.

The Centurion: He had charge of the Roman soldiers who executed Him, hear him: "Truly this was the Son of God." Matt. 27:54.

Devils: They recognized Him and bore testimony to His divinity, saying: "Jesus, thou Son of God; art thou come hither to torment us before the time." Matt. 8:29.

HIS FRIENDS.

John the Baptist: "Behold the Lamb of God which taketh away the sin of the world." John 1:29.

Peter: "Thou art the Christ, the Son of the living God." Matt. 10:16.

Thomas: "My Lord and my God." John 20:28.

Angels: "Unto you is born this day in the city of David a Savior, which is Christ the Lord." Luke 2:11.

God the Father: "And lo a voice from heaven, saying, This is my beloved Son in whom I am well pleased." Matt. 3:17.

Surely we have heard enough witnesses—whose testimony cannot be impeached—to arrive at some conclusion. "Great is the mystery * * * God was manifest in the flesh," and to this both His friends and His foes bore witness. Among a certain class we hear it said: "Christ was a good man, but not divine." This is an absurdity and a contradiction of terms. If Christ was not divine, then He was a deceiver and impostor, representing Himself to be what He was not. Surely such a one could not be termed a good man. But *He was the Son of God*.

The evidence of His divinity was manifest in His sinless life and spotless character. He could challenge even His foes to convince Him of sin. Among all the infidels in these eighteen hundred years, not one has ever found a flaw in His character. His miracles—stilling the tempest, raising the dead, curing the incurables, etc., all bear testimony to His divinity. His love and death for His enemies. His victory over death, and the grave are all in evidence of His divinity. He was God; He was man. If He was not human, then He can not be touched with the feeling of our infirmities. But He was the *God-man.* The evidences of His humanity are seen in that He was born as any other child; was partaker of flesh and blood; subject to His parents; became weary—John 4:6. Felt the pangs of sorrow.—John 11:35. Became hungry and thirsty.—Matt. 4:2; John 4:7. He knew what it was to be lonely and forsaken.—John 6:67; Matt. 8:20. "Was in all points tempted like as we are, yet without sin."

THE TEST OF GENUINE RELIGION.

Text:. *The God that answereth by fire, let Him be God.*—I. Kings 18:24.

1. THE SOURCE OF TROUBLE.

This scripture is connected with a most critical period in the history of Israel—particularly Samaria's three and a half year's drouth and subsequent calamity. The cause of their trouble was that they had "forsaken the commandments of the Lord," "and went and served Baal, and worshipped him." Sin invariably brings trouble and calamity, and the curse of God. "God is not mocked: for whatsoever a man soweth, that shall he also reap." God "will render to every man according to his deeds. * * Unto them that are contentious, and do not obey the truth, but obey unrighteousness, indignation and wrath, *tribulation* and *anguish,* upon every soul of man that doeth evil, of the Jew first, and also of the Gentile."

2. THE FAITH OF ELIJAH.

We are eager to form the acquaintance of the man who can, by his prayers, lock up the heavens so there is no dew or rain for the space of three and one-half years, and bring down the fire of God, and again unlock the heavens so that there is an abundance of rain. Elijah was one of the most rugged characters in Hebrew history. He was utterly separated from the people and entirely devoted to God; was uncompromising; yielded unfaltering obedience, was resolute and earnest; dared to stand alone; and was strong in faith. He not only trusted in God but God trusted him.

3. THE SUPREME TEST.

"The God that answereth." The religion of Jesus Christ does not consist in forms and ceremonies and mere outward morality. There must still be the manifestation of something supernatural—the answer of God. We are told not to believe every spirit. The touchstone whereby the genuine may be distinguished from the counterfeit; the false from the true, is by the power of the Gospel that saves men from sin. The salvation of the Son of God is the only thing in all the world that can save men from sin, and if a man is not saved from sinning he is not saved at all. A sinning religion is the devil's religion, and is a counterfeit, no matter what the pretenses or ritualism may be. Does the peculiar tenet or the religion you profess or believe in, save you from sin? If not, it is a farce and a delusion. His name is called Jesus because He saves his people from (not in) their sins. "He that committeth sin is of the devil. * * Whosoever is born of God doth not commit sin. * * In this the children of God are manifest and the children of the devil." This is the dividing line—the children of the devil commit sin, and the children of God do not commit sin.

4. THE FIRE.

We still have the promise of the answer by fire. "He shall baptize you with the Holy Ghost, and with fire." The fire signifies refining and purification—never pardon —and comes to God's people as a second experience, as on Pentecost. Fire penetrates, transforms, attracts, consumes, gives light, welds, is a source of power, and heat, and sets fire, There is something intense about fire, and is vastly different to much of the cold, fireless churchianity of the day. Not painted fire, nor wildfire, but Holy Ghost fire which comes from heaven; this is an actual necessity— the imperative need and glorious privilege of all Christians.

REDEEMED FROM THE CURSE OF THE LAW.

Text: *Christ hath redeemed us from the curse of the law, being made a curse for us; for it is written, Cursed is every one that hangeth on a tree; that the blessing of Abraham might come on the Gentiles through Jesus Christ; that we might receive the promise of the Spirit through faith.—Gal.* 3: 13-14.

I. THE CURSE OF THE LAW.

The curse is:—

1. *Universal*: Since "all have sinned and come short

of the glory of God." (Rom. 3:23) "The Scripture has concluded all under sin." "There is no difference."

2. *It is just*: Because God is just, and the law is just, and our sin is without excuse.

3. *It is present*: The death warrant has already been issued. The man in sin "Is condemned already."—John 3:18.

4. *It is fearful*: It includes physical, spiritual and eternal death. "It is a fearful thing to fall into the hands of the living God."—Heb. 10:31. Our only hope of escape from the curse of the law we have transgressed, is in Christ as our substitute. The law pronounces curses, but the Gospel offers blessing:

II. THE BLESSING OF ABRAHAM.

1. *It is Justification by faith*: "Abraham believed God and it was accounted to him for righteousness." He was accepted of God and accounted righteous, not because of his obedience to the law, but because of his faith. "To him that worketh not, but believeth on Him that justifieth the ungodly, his faith is counted for righteousness." (Rom. 4:5.) "Therefore we conclude that a man is justified by faith without the deeds of the law." (Rom. 3:28.)

2. *It is "come on the Gentiles."* Thus we are included. "It was not written for his sake alone, that it was imputed to him; but for us also, to whom it shall be imputed, if we believe on Him." (Rom. 4:23-24.) "Whosoever will, let him take the water of life freely." (Rev. 22:17.)

3. *Justification is instantaneouss*. The curse is re-

moved in a single moment. In the language of the poet:—

> "The moment a sinner believes,
> And trusts in his crucified God,
> His pardon at once he receives,
> Salvation in full through His blood."

iii. THE PROMISE OF THE SPIRIT.

1. *To whom given.* To believers only. Christ said, "The Spirit of truth whom the world cannot receive." (John 14:17.) Christ is the gift of God to the world; the Holy Spirit is the gift of God to the Church Hence the receiving of this promise is a second experience. "This is that which was spoken by the prophet Joel; and it shall come to pass in the last days, saith God, I will pour out of my Spirit upon all flesh." (Acts 2:16-17.)

2. *What it means.* Peter referring to Pentecost said it was the "purifying their hearts by faith." (Acts 15:8, 9.) And again we read. "Ye shall receive power, after that the Holy Ghost is come upon you; and ye shall be witnesses unto Me." Negatively stated the baptism with the Holy Ghost means *purity,* and the positive side means *power.* The failure of many is due to the fact that they want power without purity.

3. *How obtained.* By obedient faith. To the disciples it was said, "Tarry until." "God gave them the like gift." The Holy Spirit must be received as a "gift." "If ye then, being evil, know how to give good gifts unto your children; how much more shall your heavenly Father give the Holy Spirit to them that ask him." "Receive the promise of the Spirit through faith."

"FULLNESS OF JESUS."

HUNGERING AND THIRSTING.

"Blessed are they which do hunger and thirst after righteousness, for they shall be filled."—Matt. v, 6.

"Hunger" and "thirst" presuppose a spiritual birth. Being "born again" is the antecedent of spiritual hunger Adam Clarke, as other commentators, says this hunger is none other than a "desire to be holy," and this "righteousness" signifying "the full salvation of God." Hunger is an evidence of life, and a good appetite and relish for spiritual things an evidence of a healthful condition. The condition for filling is the emptying and purifying process. The great reason all are not filled is because they do not consent to be emptied first. "Shall be filled!"

ASK, AND RECEIVE.

"Ask, and ye shall receive, that your joy may be full."—John 16:24.

Thrice, within the very shadow of the cross, the Savior gave expression to this yearning of His heart that the disciple should have fullness of joy. (John xv, 11; John xvi, 24; John xvii, 13.) All Christians have a measure of joy; but all Christians do not have the fullness of joy. This is one distinction between justification and sanctification. "Rejoice in the Lord alway." Not spasmodic and sporadic joy, but constant and abiding fullness of joy is the privilege of the believer. "Joy unspeakable and full of glory." (1 Peter i, 8.) "The joy of the Lord is your strength." (Neh. viii, 10.) "I will yet for this be enquired of." (Exek. xxxvi, 37.)

WITH THE SPIRIT.

"And they were all filled with the Holy Ghost,"—Acts ii, 4.

A statement concerning one hundred and twenty Christians who lived a long time ago, the result of which was three thousand conversions in one day. Some have supposed that it required ten days to get "filled." It took them ten days to become thoroughly emptied of self, when, lo, the Spirit cleansed and filled them "suddenly" and instantaneously. "The Lord, whom ye seek, shall suddenly come to His temple." (Mal. iii, 1.) First. They were obedient in going and tarrying at Jerusalem. Second. They were united, of one mind and one accord. Third. They were in one place. Fourth. They were expectant. "Suddenly there came a sound from heaven." (Acts ii, 2.)

ABOVE MEASURE.

"God giveth not the Spirit by measure."—John iii, 34.

So every one may have according to his capacity and need. Great difficulties and trials simply open up avenues for a larger supply and manifestations of the Spirit, since God has said, "As thy days, so shall thy strength be." (Deut. xxxiii, 25.) Great trials make way for great grace. The idea that a soul can only hold out and triumph under favorable circumstances and pleasing environments is utterly false. "As ye are partakers of the sufferings, so shall ye be also of the consolation." (2 Cor. i, 7.) "Thou preparest a table before me in the presence of mine enemies: Thou anointest my head with oil: my cup runneth over." (Ps. xxiii, 5.)

FILLED.

"Be filled with the Spirit."—Eph. v, 18.

This is the privilege and duty of every believer. God's "Be" is imperative, and must not be regarded as optional. No excuse can be allowed for a lack of the fullness of the Spirit since "the promise is unto you,.... even as many as the Lord our God shall call." (Acts ii, 39.) This filling marks a distinct crisis or epoch in the life of all who receive it. It is an experience subsequent to regeneration. The Spirit is never promised nor given to an unregenerated heart. "The Spirit of truth, whom the world can not receive." (John xiv, 17.)

BLESSINGS POURED OUT.

"Bring ye all the tithes into the storehouse, and prove Me now herewith, saith the Lord of Hosts, if I will not open you the windows of heaven, and pour you out (marg. empty out) a blessing that there shall not be room enough to receive it."—Mal. iii, 10.

Tithing is simply discharging our financial obligation to God. This is God's own method for meeting all expenses of the Church He Himself instituted. Where tithing is faithfully observed, there is no occasion for adopting questionable, claptrap methods of money raising. Every financial difficulty is solved, the financial burden equalized, as all pay alike, and great blessing and prosperity—both spiritual and temporal—is at once assured. "Give, and it shall be given you: good measure, pressed down, and shaken together, and running over." (Luke vi. 38.)

FULL OF SAP.

"The trees of the Lord are full of sap."—Ps. civ. 16.

The flowing sap is ever an evidence of life, and denotes a healthful, thrifty condition. According to the parable of the sower and the seed, some Christians die spiritually for want of moisture. (Luke viii, 6.) There is a vast difference between a dry, formal religion and a religion full of sap; an experience that has some juice and gravy to it. What the sap is to a tree the fullness of the Spirit is to the Christian. "To give unto them beauty for ashes, the oil of joy for mourning, the garments of praise for the spirit of heaviness; that they might be called trees of righteousness." (Isaiah lxi, 3.)

FULL OF LIGHT.

"The light of the body is the eye; if therefore thine eye be single, thy whole body shall be full of light."—Matt. vi, 22.

Light is a synonym of knowledge. The "single eye" denotes singleness of purpose—seeking only the glory of God. Spiritual knowledge is conditioned upon obedience. "If any man will do His will, he shall know of the doctrine." (John vii. 17.) "God is light, and in Him is no darkness at all. If we say we have fellowship with Him, and walk in darkness, we lie, and do not the truth." (John i, 5, 6.) "Light is sown for the righteous." (Ps. xcvii, 11.) "If we walk in the light as He is in the light, we have fellowship one with another, and the blood of Jesus Christ His Son cleanseth us from all sin." (1 John i, 7.) "Truly the light is sweet." (Eccl. xi, 7.) "The path of the just is as the shining light, that shineth more and more unto the perfect day." (Prov. iv, 18.)

FILLED WITH GOD'S FULLNESS.

"And to know the love of Christ which passeth knowledge, that ye might be filled with all the fullness of God."—Eph. iii, 19.

Being filled with all the fullness of God is sharply conditioned upon first knowing "the love of Christ," which itself passeth all human knowledge, and can only be known as revealed by the Spirit. "That ye might be filled." Of what is God full? He is full of light, life, joy, power, glory, etc., and we shall be filled with exactly the same. Surely this will exclude everything else. A cup may be just as certainly filled, and filled with exactly the same water as is found in the ocean; while there is no difference in the quality, there is a world of difference in the quantity.

FILLED BY FAITH.

"The God of hope fill you with all joy and peace in believing."—Rom. xv, 13.

Peace and joy come by believing. Where faith is triumphant, joy is full, and peace passeth understanding. Doubt brings unrest and consequent despondency and gloom. "Thou wilt keep him in perfect peace, whose mind is stayed on Thee: because he trusteth in Thee." (Isaiah xxvi, 3.) "In whom, though now ye see Him not, yet believing, ye rejoice with joy unspeakable and full of glory." (1 Peter i, 8.) "According to your faith be it unto you." (Matt. ix, 29.) We can not know peace and joy by trying to feel them—but by believing God.

FULL OF POWER.

"But truly I am full of power by the Spirit of the Lord."—Micah iii, 8.

A fullness of the Spirit is the Divine order and secret of power. The Pentecostal blessing first purifies (Acts xv, 8, 9,), and then empowers for service. Without heart-purity there can be no genuine Pentecostal power. It is power, first, to cease from all sin; second, power to endure patiently and victoriously, as "seeing Him that is invisible," amid temptation and trial; third, power to execute and perform the whole will of God. It requires more power to keep sweet and patient under trial than to do some powerful shouting during big meetings. "But ye shall receive power, after that the Holy Ghost is come upon you." (Acts i, 8.)

FRUITS OF RIGHTEOUSNESS.

"Being filled with the fruits of righteousness, which are by Jesus Christ, unto the glory and praise of God."—Phil. i, 11.

There is a difference between works and fruit. Many have good works, who, nevertheless, have not the Spirit, and so necessarily are destitute of the fruits of the Spirit. Works may be the result of mere human effort, while fruit is spontaneous—the result of spiritual life. "The fruit of the Spirit is love, joy, peace, long-suffering, gentleness, goodness, faith, meekness, temperance," (Gal. v, 22.) "Herein is my Father glorified that ye bear much fruit; so shall ye be My disciples." (John xv, 8.) "Every branch in Me that beareth not fruit, He taketh away." (John xv, 2.)

FULL OF GOODNESS.

"Ye also are full of goodness."—Rom. xv, 14.

While "there is none that doeth good, no, not one," in his unrenewed and unregenerate state, it is also true that Jesus Christ can take a bad man and make a good man out of him. We read, Luke xxiii, 50; "Joseph.... was a good man;" and Acts xi, 24, we read of Barnabas: "He was a good man." So, according to these Scriptures, at least two good men have lived on the face of the earth. And if these men could be made into good men, then, by the grace of God, others may. "A good man sheweth favor." (Ps. cxii, 5.) Surely Jesus can not say "Well done, thou good and faithful servant" (Matt. xxv, 21), if we have not been good. Thank God for the transforming power of grace!

FILLED WITH FOOD.

"When thou has eaten and art full, then thou shalt bless the Lord thy God."—Deut. viii, 10.

There is no excuse for God's saints to be lean, weak, and half starved. "He satisfieth the longing soul, and filleth the hungry soul with goodness." (Ps. cvii, 9.) When the heart is filled, the next thing on the program is to "bless the Lord." "Praise is comely for the upright." (Ps. xxxiii, 1.) "Whoso offereth praise glorifieth Me." (Ps. l, 23.) The overflowing blessing is necessary to refresh those about us; the little we can hold we need for ourselves. "Eat ye that which is good, and let your soul delight itself in fatness." (Isaiah lv, 2.) He "filleth thee with the finest of the wheat." (Ps. clvii, 14.

GOD'S FULLNESS.

"And of His fullness have all we received, and grace for grace."—John i, 16.

No experience of grace should be regarded as a finality; as though we had received all; rather, every experience should be recognized as a stepping-stone to higher altitudes of grace. Grace prepares us for the reception of more grace. The grace of justification prepares us for the grace of entire sanctification. Entire sanctification prepares us for glorification. No matter what our present experience, there is always more to follow. "It is better farther on." "He is able to do exceeding abundantly above all that we ask or think."

FULL OF WISDOM.

"And Joshua, the son of Nun, was full of the spirit of wisdom."—Deut. xxxiv, 9.

God places no premium on ignorance, although He "made foolish the wisdom of this world." (1 Cor. i, 20.) Men can not be guilty of greater folly than when they substitute the wisdom of this world for the Holy Ghost. God can not be found out by the wisdom of this world. Things that are spiritual can only be known as revealed by the Holy Spirit. "The fear of the Lord is the beginning of wisdom." (Prov. ix, 10.) "The wisdom that is from above is first pure, then peaceable, gentle, and easy to be entreated, full of mercy and good fruits." (James iii, 17.) "If any of you lack wisdom, let him ask of God, that giveth to all men liberally, and upbraideth not; and it shall be given him." (James i, 5.)

FULLNESS OF THE BLESSING.

"I am sure that when I come unto you, I shall come in the fullness of the blessing of the gospel of Christ."—Rom. xv, 29.

Before a minister can be sure that he will come to his people in the fullness of the blessing, he must be sure he has the fullness of the blessing. There is a blessing and "the fullness of the blessing," just as there is "life," and "life more abundant." The "fullness of the blessing" excludes everything else from the heart. Where unholy ambition, self-will, pride, doubt, and a man-fearing and man-pleasing spirit is found, "the fullness of blessing" is not. The fact that there may be some water in the pitcher is not an evidence that the pitcher is full of water. "Of His fullness have all we received, and grace for grace." (John i, 16.)

MOUTHS FILLED.

"Open thy mouth wide, and I will fill it."—Ps. lxxxi, 10.

The "mouth," "tongue," and "conversation" are an index to the heart. "How can ye, being evil, speak good things? for out of the abundance of the heart the mouth speaketh." (Matt. xii, 34.) God fills the mouth by first filling the heart. A full heart brings the ringing testimony. "They were all filled with the Holy Ghost, and began to speak." (Acts ii, 4.) The Pentecostal blessing is always the "speaking blessing." "I will give you a mouth and wisdom, which all your adversaries shall not be able to gainsay nor resist." (Luke xxi, 15,) "With the mouth confession is made unto salvation." (Rom. x, 10.)

FULLNESS OF THE GODHEAD.

"For in Him dwelleth all the fullness of the Godhead bodily."—Col. ii, 9.

Everything pertaining to present and eternal salvation is found in Christ Jesus. He is the "Light," the "Life," the "Truth," the "Way," the "Door," and, "of God, is made unto us wisdom, and righteousness, and sanctification, and redemption." (1 Cor. i, 30.) In Him you may find your every need supplied. "Christ in everything, and everything in Christ," should be the motto of every Christian, "till we all come in the unity of the faith and the knowledge of the Son of God, unto a perfect man, unto the measure of the stature of the fullness of Christ." (Eph. iv, 13.)

GOOD MEASURE.

"Give, and it shall be given unto you; good measure, pressed down, and shaken together, and running over, shall men give into your bosom. For with the same measure that ye mete withal it shall be measured to you again."—Luke vi, 38.

It is well to remember that it is not the stingy and close-fisted soul, but "the liberal soul shall be made fat." (Prov. xi, 24.) Liberality insures temporal success and prosperity. Many of God's people are poverty-stricken, simply because they are miserly. "There is that scattereth, and yet increaseth; and there is that withholdeth more than is meet; but it tendeth to poverty." (Prov. xi, 24.) "He which soweth sparingly shall reap also sparingly; and he which soweth bountifully shall reap also bountifully." (2 Cor. ix, 6.)

FULL OF TEMPORAL BLESSINGS.

"He maketh peace in thy borders, and filleth thee with the finest of the wheat."—Ps. cxlvii, 14.

The marginal rendering is "the fat of the wheat." God intends His people should have the best He has in store. Then why should any live on skimmed milk when they might have the cream; or live on half rations when they might have a full meal? or ask for crumbs when God desires to give you the whole loaf? Peace and plenty is the heritage of all who will obey Him. "He should have fed them also with the finest of the wheat; and with honey out of the Rock should I have satisfied thee." Ps. lxxxi, 16.) "If ye be willing and obedient, ye shall eat the good of the land." (Isaiah i, 19.)

FILLED WITH KNOWLEDGE.

"Filled with all knowledge, able also to admonish one another."—Rom. xv, 14.

The knowledge which the Bible commends is an experimental knowledge. Theoretical knowledge may be gathered from books, and is simply a thing of the head; experimental knowledge can only be obtained at the feet of Jesus, as revealed by the Spirit, and is a thing of the heart. "Now we have received . . . the Spirit which is of God, that we might know the things that are freely given to us of God." (1 Cor. ii, 12.) Things hidden from the wise and prudent are "revealed" unto babes." (Luke x, 21.) "God gave them knowledge and skill in all learning and wisdom." (Dan. i, 17.) "In whom are hid all the treasures of wisdom and knowledge."

FULL OF GOOD WORKS.

"This woman was full of good works and almsdeeds which she did."—Acts ix, 36.

What a desirable epitaph for a saint of God who has departed this life! What an index to character! "This woman" spoken of was Dorcas, whose post-office address was Joppa. Good works will not secure for us the favor of God; but "good works" are the inevitable result of faith and favor in God. They are not so much the result of effort as they are the expression of a good heart. However poor in this world's goods, the person filled with the Spirit of Christ will have a liberal spirit and find opportunity to give some alms. "Faith without works is dead." (James ii, 26.)

THE HUNGRY ARE FILLED.

"He satisfieth the longing soul, and filleth the hungry soul with goodness."—Ps. cvii, 9.

No one should rest in an experience that does not give entire satifsaction: for the experience that does not fully satisfy the longing of the human heart never satisfies God. By awakening deeper desires, and a hungering and thirsting in the soul, God means to lead us into higher heights and deeper depths of His love. Satisfaction is guaranteed to all who will abide in the center of His will. When Christians follow the things of the world they plainly say their religion does not satisfy. "They shall be abundantly satisfied with the fatness of thy house; and thou shalt make them drink of the river of thy pleasures." (Ps. xxxvi, 8.) "The meek shall eat and be satisfied." (Ps. xxii, 26.)

FILLED WITH JOY.

"Thou shalt make me full of joy with thy countenance."
—Acts ii, 28.

True happiness is not conditioned on what we have, but rather on what we are. A glimpse of Jesus will always enrapture and ravish the soul with delight.

> "As by the light of opening day,
>   The stars are all concealed;
> So earthly pleasures fade away,
>   When Jesus is revealed."

"In Thy presence is fullness of joy." (Ps. xvi, 8.) "The kingdom of God is . . . righteousness, and peace, and joy in the Holy Ghost." (Rom. xiv, 17.) According to this analysis, one-third of religion is joy. "In whom, though now ye see Him not, yet believing, ye rejoice with joy unspeakable and full of glory." (1 Peter i, 8.)

www.ingramcontent.com/pod-product-compliance
Lightning Source LLC
Chambersburg PA
CBHW071446150426
43191CB00008B/1254